—FAVORITE HOMEMADE—
COOKIES AND CANDIES

SEDGEWOOD PRESS

Published by Sedgewood Press

For Sedgewood Press
Editorial Director: Jane Ross
Supervising Editor: Gale Kremer
Production Manager: Bill Rose

Produced for Sedgewood Press by
Marshall Cavendish House
58 Old Compton Street
LONDON W1V 4PA

For Marshall Cavendish
Consultant Editor: Virginia Colton
American Editor: Norma MacMillan
Designer: Brenda Morrison

First printing 1982

Library of Congress Cataloging in Publication
Data
1. Non-fiction
2. Cooking

LCCN 81-71015
Distributed in the Trade by Van Nostrand Reinhold
ISBN 0-442-28089-0

Printed in the United States of America

PICTURE CREDITS
Bryce Attwell: 43 (t)
Paul Bussell: 79 (t), 91
Camera Press: 178, 179, 183
John Cooke: 111
Delu/PAF International: 147 (b)
Alan Duns: 23, 27, 35, 63, 67, 82, 99, 142, 171
Melvin Grey: 131 (b), 163 (b), 182
Anthony Kay: 51, 55, 87, 122
Paul Kemp: 6, 59, 79 (b), 123
David Levin: 15, 19, 134/5, 150/1, 154, 158, 159 (1),
166, 190, 191
Frederick Mancini: 155, 159 (r)
Roger Phillips: 22, 31, 39, 43 (b), 47, 54, 71 (t), 75,
95 (b), 119, 139, 143, 147 (t), 174
Nick Powell: 114/15, 167
Iain Reid: 10, 71 (b), 95 (t)
Paul Williams: 14, 102, 106, 127, 131 (t), 163 (t), 187

ILLUSTRATIONS
Victoria Drew: 178, 182
All black and white line drawings by Anne Morrow

INTRODUCTION

There's nothing like the aroma of freshly baked cookies and homemade candies to bring back childhood memories—the kind of memories we want to share with our children, and hope they'll pass on to theirs.

FAVORITE HOMEMADE COOKIES AND CANDIES restores those sweet scents of yesterday to our kitchens of today, with a mouthwatering collection of can't-miss recipes for those delicious cookies and candies you remember so fondly. Its easy-to-follow format and plentiful color photographs turn cookie- and candy-making into pure pleasure for the whole family—great fun, and unbelievably good eating. Old favorites such as Butterscotch Brownies, Spiced Molasses Cookies, Divinity and Rocky Road join such newer temptations as Funny Faces, No-bake Orange Mocha Bars and Chocolate Easter Eggs to guarantee textures and flavors to everyone's taste. And there's a special section devoted to "Super" cookies and candies, among them the makings of a gingerbread castle and a log cabin, and some marvelous Christmas tree cookies that look too beautiful to eat (but eaten they will be!).

FAVORITE HOMEMADE COOKIES AND CANDIES really *is* what so many books claim to be: an all-time family classic.

CONTENTS COOKIES

CANDIES

COOKIES

A cookie jar full of home-baked bars, drops or other treats is every homemaker's pride — and every child's dream. There can be no better after-school snack than cookies and milk, and what picnic or packed lunch, coffee break or tea party, or even a special company dinner would be complete without cookies you have made yourself?

Your children or grandchildren may like to help you in the kitchen, and they'll love baking cookies. Mixing the dough, rolling it out and cutting out different shapes are fun to do, as well as being instructive for budding cooks.

A selection of delicious cookies (clockwise): Sugar Cookies (page 44) made with special shapes and decorated to taste; Lemon Cookies (page 45) decorated with chocolate frosting and flaked almonds; Fudge Butter Bars (page 49), Orange Shortbread (page 32) and Spiced Raspberry Cookies (page 20).

Chapter One

BASIC INFORMATION

Ingredients

Flour: Most recipes call for all-purpose flour, which may be either regular or quick-mixing. Those recipes that use self-rising flour, or a mixture of self-rising and all-purpose, will produce a softer cookie with a more cake-like texture. Whole wheat flour is also sometimes called for; if you use stone-ground whole wheat flour, the cookies will have a coarser texture.

Fat: Butter or margarine are most often used in the recipes in this book. Use the stick type, not whipped. If you want to substitute shortening, use the solid hydrogenated type sold in cans. Do not substitute oil for solid fats.

Eggs: Use medium-size eggs unless the recipe specifies large. If possible, have the eggs at room temperature.

Baking powder: Use double-action baking powder in all recipes.

Sweeteners: Granulated, confectioner's and brown sugar, honey, corn syrup and molasses are all used in cookie-making.

Flavorings: These include finely grated orange or lemon rind, vanilla and almond extract, spices, unsweetened cocoa (unless sweetened hot chocolate powder is specified), or chocolate. This is where your own imagination can take over, and new cookie variations be invented.

Other ingredients: Nuts, fresh and dried fruits, jam, chocolate chips, granola and other breakfast cereals, oats, coconut, cream cheese . . . the list is endless.

Utensils

Apart from a mixing bowl, electric or rotary beater (or wooden spoon if you're energetic), and rolling pin, there are few special utensils required for making cookies. If you have a food processor, it can be used to make cookie dough in seconds. Follow the manufacturer's instructions.

Cookie cutters: Metal cutters give a cleaner cut than plastic ones. If you don't have cutters of the right shape or size, drinking glasses make a useful standby. Dip all cutters in flour before using.

TESTER'S TIP

Even if the pack specifies that a flour has been sifted, always sift again before adding to other ingredients. Don't sift whole wheat flour otherwise you'll sift out the grains — just stir and mix in.

Almond Chocolate Chip Cookies (page 34)

Cookie press: This convenient device eliminates rolling out the dough and cutting individual cookies by hand. The wide hollow tube is filled with cookie dough; a plunger forces it out through a shaped plate at the other end. Keep the dough pliable to obtain well-defined patterns, and chill the dough if it becomes soft. For softer doughs, a pastry bag is often easier to use.

Cookie sheets: These should be shiny and at least 2 inches narrower and shorter than your oven so the heat can circulate around them. Grease the cookie sheets — with unsalted butter or shortening — only if the recipe specifies, and if possible work with two cookie sheets: fill one while the other is in the oven. Place dough on a cool cookie sheet: the dough will spread if the cookie sheet is hot. Baking or jelly roll pans are used for baking bars. They are usually square (8 inch or 9 inch size) or rectangular (11×7, 12×8, 13×9 or $15\frac{1}{2} \times 10\frac{1}{2}$ inches).

Wire rack: Cool cookies on a wire rack so that air can circulate all around them. This will prevent sogginess. Remember that the cookies will continue to cook on the cookie sheet after it is removed from the oven, so follow the recipe timing for removing the cookies, using a wide spatula.

Cookies can be baked in a microwave oven, but they cook so quickly that there is little or no browning. If you want to use a microwave, choose a cookie dough that is dark, such as chocolate or spice, or a bar or cookie that will be frosted after baking.

TESTER'S TIP

Measure all dry ingredients in special dry measuring cups for complete accuracy; DO NOT use liquid measuring cups. Dry measurements are level, not rounded. Measure all liquid ingredients at eye level.

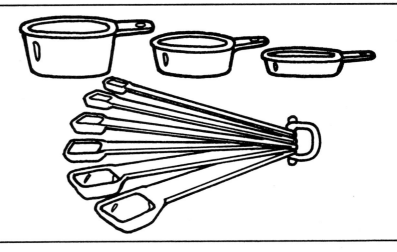

Types of Cookies

There are basically five kinds of cookies, each made a slightly different way. For **rolled cookies,** the dough is rolled out on a lightly floured surface with a floured rolling pin (or one wrapped in stockinette) and then cut into shapes. Chilling the dough before rolling will prevent sticking. Cut the cookies as close together as possible to avoid re-rolling because the dough when rolled out again will be much drier due to the extra flour worked in. Lift the cookies onto a cookie sheet with a spatula.

Drop cookies usually have a softer dough than that for rolled cookies. The dough is scooped up with a tableware teaspoon or tablespoon and then pushed onto a cookie sheet with a second spoon. These cookies tend to spread a lot during baking, so leave plenty of room around each one on the cookie sheet. Try to make each cookie the same size so that they'll all bake in the same time. Some recipes specify flattening the cookie before baking; this is usually done with a fork or the heel of your hand.

Molded cookies are shaped into balls, triangles, crescents, pretzels, knots, twists or other decorative shapes, sometimes using special molds or a cookie press. The dough is often quite stiff to make the shaping easier. Molded cookies may be coated in coconut, sugar, chopped nuts, etc., or molded around a nut, candy or candied cherry.

TESTER'S TIP

Preheat the oven for at least 10 minutes before you put the cookies in to bake. Either put the sheet into the center of the oven or arrange your oven into thirds so that you can bake two sheets at once. If you can't, cook one sheet at a time for best results.

For **refrigerator cookies** the rich dough is chilled to make it firm enough to slice with a sharp knife. This cookie dough can be kept in the refrigerator for up to 6 weeks (or 5–6 months in the freezer) so cookies may be sliced off and baked when wanted. To speed the chilling of the dough before baking, it may be placed in the freezer.

For **bars,** the dough is pressed into a pan, baked and then cut into bars, fingers or squares. Use the exact size pan specified in the recipe: a larger pan will give a dry, brittle result and a pan that is too small will make the bars too cake-like.

Filled cookies are rolled or molded cookies or bars that are baked and then put together in pairs with jam, sweetened whipped cream, buttercream frosting or some other delicious concoction.

Storing Cookies

Store soft cookies in a tightly covered jar or other container. Crisp cookies should be kept in a container with a loose-fitting lid to retain freshness. If they soften, they can be crisped in a 300° oven for 3–5 minutes. Bars can be kept, covered with foil, in the pan in which they were baked.

For longer storage, freeze cookies. Frosted cookies will keep for 2–3 months, and unfrosted cookies for 9–12 months. To thaw, place the cookies on a plate and leave at room temperature for about 20 minutes.

TESTER'S TIP

Remember to let your cookies cool before you eat them — they firm up and crisp during the cooling process.

Making Rolled Cookies Step by Step

1. Preheat the oven to the temperature specified in the recipe. Grease a cookie sheet.
2. Sift the flour, salt and any spices into a bowl. Cut in the fat until the mixture resembles crumbs. Stir in the sugar and any other dry ingredients.

3. Add the egg and/or any other liquid and mix to a smooth dough.
4. Roll out the dough on a floured surface with a floured rolling pin to the thickness specified in the recipe.

5. Dip the cookie cutter in flour, then cut out the shapes desired. Arrange on the cookie sheet.
6. Prick each cookie with a fork or glaze, as the recipe directs. Bake for the required time.
Let the cookies cool slightly on the cookie sheet—they will be soft, but will firm up as they cool. Remove to a wire rack to cool completely.

Drop Cookies and Bars Step by Step

1. Preheat the oven to the temperature specified in the recipe. Grease a cookie sheet. Cream the fat with a wooden spoon until softened, then beat in the sugar until the mixture is light and fluffy.

2. Alternatively, beat the fat and sugar together with an electric mixer. Beat in the eggs.

3. Sift in the flour, spices and other dry ingredients and mix well.

4. Drop by rounded teaspoonfuls onto the cookie sheet. Use another teaspoon to help, and leave plenty of room for spreading on the cookie sheet. Flatten the cookies with the heel of your hand or a fork if the recipe directs.

5. For bars, press the cookie dough evenly over the bottom of a greased square or rectangular pan. Make sure the corners are filled.

6. Mark into bars before or after baking, as specified in the recipe.

Chapter Two

FAMILY FAVORITES

Sand Tarts

MAKES ABOUT 2 DOZEN

½ cup butter or margarine
1½ cups sugar
1 egg
½ teaspoon vanilla
1¾ cups all-purpose flour
1 teaspoon baking powder
¼ teaspoon salt
1 egg white, beaten until frothy
¼ teaspoon ground cinnamon
walnut or blanched almond halves

Cream the butter or margarine with 1¼ cups of the sugar until light and fluffy. Beat in the egg and vanilla. Sift the flour, baking powder and salt into the bowl and mix to a firm dough. Refrigerate for 1 hour.

Preheat the oven to 350°.

Roll out the dough on a floured surface to about ¼ inch thick. Cut into shapes with floured cookie cutters. Arrange on greased cookie sheets.

Brush the shapes with the egg white. Mix the remaining sugar with the cinnamon and sprinkle over the tops. Press a walnut or almond half into each cookie.

Bake for 15–20 minutes or until lightly browned around the edges. Let cool on the cookie sheets for 5 minutes, then remove to a wire rack to cool completely.

Icicles

MAKES ABOUT 1½ DOZEN

4 tablespoons butter or margarine
¼ cup sugar
¾ cup all-purpose flour
¼ cup cornstarch
3 tablespoons water
½ teaspoon vanilla
3 tablespoons apricot jam
1 teaspoon lemon juice
MERINGUE
2 egg whites
½ cup sugar

Preheat the oven to 350°.

Cream the butter or margarine with the sugar until light and fluffy. Sift the flour and cornstarch into the bowl and mix well. Add the water and vanilla and mix to a soft dough.

Roll out the dough on a floured surface to about ¼ inch thick. Cut out 1½ inch rounds and arrange on a greased cookie sheet. Bake for 8 minutes or until light golden brown.

Meanwhile, make the meringue. Beat the egg whites until stiff. Add 1 tablespoon of the sugar and beat for a further 1 minute or until the meringue is very stiff and glossy. Fold in the remaining sugar with a metal spoon.

Remove the cookies from the oven and let cool slightly.

Mix the jam with the lemon juice. Place a small spoonful of the jam in the center of each cookie. Put the meringue into a pastry bag fitted with a ½ inch star tip and pipe in swirls on top of the cookies to cover them completely.

Return to the oven and bake for 8 minutes longer or until the meringue is set and lightly browned. Cool on the cookie sheet.

Snickerdoodles

MAKES ABOUT 2 DOZEN

½ cup butter or margarine
¾ cup sugar
1 egg
1½ cups all-purpose flour
½ teaspoon baking soda
½ teaspoon cream of tartar
⅛ teaspoon salt
1 tablespoon ground cinnamon

Preheat the oven to 375°.

Cream the butter or margarine with ½ cup of the sugar until light and fluffy. Beat in the egg. Sift the flour, soda, cream of tartar and salt into the bowl and mix to a smooth dough.

Mix together the cinnamon and remaining sugar on a plate.

Roll the dough into walnut-size balls and coat with the cinnamon mixture. Arrange on ungreased cookie sheets, leaving room for spreading, and flatten the balls with the heel of your hand.

Bake for 10–12 minutes or until lightly browned and firm to the touch. Let cool on the cookie sheets for 5 minutes, then remove to a wire rack to cool completely.

Cream Cheese and Walnut Cookies

MAKES 2 DOZEN

1 pkg (8 oz) cream cheese
1 cup butter or margarine
2 cups all-purpose flour
¼ cup sugar
1 teaspoon ground cinnamon
2 tablespoons raisins
2 tablespoons chopped candied fruit
  peel
½ cup finely chopped walnuts
20 walnut halves

Beat the cream cheese and butter or margarine together. Sift the flour into the bowl and mix to a soft dough. Refrigerate for 1 hour.

Meanwhile, mix together the sugar, cinnamon, raisins, fruit peel and chopped walnuts.

Preheat the oven to 350°.

Roll the cream cheese dough into 24 balls. Make a deep indentation in each with your thumb and fill with the fruit and nut mixture. Pinch the edges of the balls together to seal in the filling and press a walnut half into the top of each.

Arrange the balls on a greased baking sheet, leaving room for spreading. Bake for 15–20 minutes or until golden brown. Cool on a wire rack.

Currant Cookies

MAKES 2½ DOZEN

10 tablespoons butter or margarine
grated rind of 1 lemon
½ cup + 1 tablespoon sugar
1 egg
1 egg, separated
2 cups all-purpose flour
pinch of salt
⅓ cup currants

Cream the butter or margarine with the lemon rind and ½ cup of sugar until light and fluffy. Beat in the whole egg and the extra egg yolk. Sift the flour and salt into the bowl and mix in. Stir in the currants. Refrigerate for 1 hour.

Preheat the oven to 375°.

Roll out the dough on a floured surface to ¼ inch thick. Cut out rounds using a floured 2 inch fluted cookie cutter. Arrange the rounds on greased cookie sheets.

Beat the remaining egg white until frothy. Brush the egg white over the cookies and sprinkle with the remaining sugar. Bake for about 15 minutes or until golden brown. Let cool on the cookie sheets for 5 minutes, then remove to a wire rack to cool completely.

Currant Cookies

Burnt Butter Cookies

MAKES ABOUT 2½ DOZEN

½ cup butter or margarine
½ cup sugar
1 large egg
1½ cups self-rising flour, sifted
15 blanched almonds, halved
   lengthwise

Preheat the oven to 350°.

Place the butter or margarine in a saucepan. Melt over low heat until pale golden. Remove from the heat and stir in the sugar until dissolved. Beat in the egg, followed by the flour.

Drop by rounded teaspoonfuls onto greased cookie sheets, leaving room for spreading. Place an almond half on each cookie.

Bake for 12–15 minutes or until golden. Let cool on the cookie sheets for 5 minutes, then remove to a wire rack to cool completely.

Spiced Raspberry Cookies

MAKES ABOUT 2 DOZEN

1¼ cups self-rising flour
¼ teaspoon ground cinnamon
¼ teaspoon ground cloves
½ cup butter or margarine
6 tablespoons sugar
1 egg
3 tablespoons milk or water
¼ cup raspberry jam
2 tablespoons confectioner's sugar

Preheat the oven to 350°.

Sift the flour and spices into a bowl. Cut in the butter or margarine until the mixture resembles fine crumbs. Stir in the sugar. Add the egg and milk or water and mix to a soft dough.

Roll out the dough on a floured surface and cut out 2½ inch rounds. Place half the rounds on greased cookie sheets.

Using a small decorative cookie cutter, cut out a shape from the center of the remaining rounds. Arrange these on greased cookie sheets.

Bake for 10–12 minutes or until pale golden. Let cool on the cookie sheets for 5 minutes, then remove to a wire rack to cool completely.

Spread the jam over the whole cookie rounds and place the cut-out rounds on top so the jam shows through. Sprinkle with the confectioner's sugar.

Refrigerator Spice Cookies

MAKES ABOUT 3 DOZEN

4 tablespoons butter or margarine
½ cup sugar
1 egg
1 teaspoon vanilla
1½ cups all-purpose flour
½ teaspoon baking soda
⅛ teaspoon salt
1 teaspoon ground cinnamon
½ teaspoon ground cloves

Cream the butter or margarine with the sugar until light and fluffy. Beat in the egg and vanilla. Sift the flour, soda, salt and spices into the bowl and mix to a firm dough.

Shape the dough into a roll about 2 inches in diameter and wrap in wax paper. Refrigerate for 2 hours (or store in the refrigerator for up to 1 week).

Preheat the oven to 375°.

Cut the roll of dough into ¼ inch thick slices and arrange on ungreased cookie sheets. Bake for 8–10 minutes or until lightly browned around the edges and firm to the touch. Let cool on the cookie sheets for 5 minutes, then remove to a wire rack to cool completely.

Carrot Cookies

MAKES ABOUT 2½ DOZEN

¾ cup butter or margarine
¾ cup sugar
grated rind of 1 orange
1 egg
3 large carrots, grated (about 1 cup)
2¼ cups all-purpose flour
½ teaspoon salt
2 teaspoons baking powder

Preheat the oven to 375°.

Cream the butter or margarine, sugar and orange rind together until light and fluffy. Beat in the egg, then the carrots. Sift the flour, salt and baking powder into the bowl and mix well.

Drop by rounded teaspoonfuls onto greased cookie sheets, leaving space for spreading. Bake for 12–15 minutes or until lightly browned around the edges. Cool on a wire rack.

Filbert Spirals

MAKES ABOUT 3 DOZEN

1 cup butter or margarine
1 cup sugar
1 egg
1 teaspoon vanilla
2½ cups all-purpose flour
½ teaspoon baking powder
¼ teaspoon grated nutmeg
¾ cup ground filberts
1 tablespoon confectioner's sugar

Preheat the oven to 350°.

Cream the butter or margarine with the sugar until light and fluffy. Beat in the egg and vanilla. Sift the flour, baking powder, nutmeg and filberts into the bowl and mix well.

Put the cookie dough into a pastry bag fitted with a ½ inch plain tip. Pipe in spirals onto greased cookie sheets. Bake for 10–15 minutes or until just firm to the touch and golden brown around the edges.

Let cool on the cookie sheets for 5 minutes, then remove to a wire rack to cool completely. Sprinkle with the confectioner's sugar before serving.

Filbert Spirals

Hermits

MAKES ABOUT 4 DOZEN

1 cup butter or margarine
1 cup firmly packed brown sugar
2 eggs
½ cup strong black coffee
2 cups all-purpose flour
1 teaspoon ground cinnamon
½ teaspoon grated nutmeg
½ teaspoon baking powder
½ cup raisins
½ cup chopped walnuts

Preheat the oven to 375°.

Cream the butter or margarine with the sugar until light and fluffy. Beat in the eggs one at a time, then beat in the coffee. Sift the flour, spices and baking powder into the bowl and beat until the mixture is smooth. Stir in the raisins and walnuts.

Drop by rounded teaspoonfuls onto greased cookie sheets, leaving room for spreading. Bake for 10–15 minutes or until golden brown. Cool on a wire rack.

Hermits

Chocolate Crinkles

MAKES ABOUT 4 DOZEN

½ cup butter or margarine
1⅔ cups sugar
2 squares (1 oz each) unsweetened
    chocolate, melted
2 eggs
1 teaspoon vanilla
2 cups all-purpose flour
¼ teaspoon baking soda
1½ teaspoons baking powder
½ teaspoon salt
6 tablespoons milk
about ½ cup confectioner's sugar

Cream the butter or margarine with the sugar until light and fluffy. Beat in the melted chocolate, then the eggs and vanilla. Sift the flour, baking soda, baking powder and salt into the bowl. Add the milk and mix well. Refrigerate for at least 2 hours.

Preheat the oven to 350°.

Roll the dough into walnut-size balls and coat with the confectioner's sugar. Arrange on greased cookie sheets, leaving room for spreading. Bake for about 12 minutes or until just firm to the touch.

Let cool on the cookie sheets for 5 minutes, then remove to a wire rack to cool completely.

Gingerbread Bites

MAKES ABOUT 2 DOZEN

3 cups all-purpose flour
1 tablespoon ground ginger
½ teaspoon baking soda
¼ cup chopped mixed candied fruit
    peel
⅔ cup firmly packed brown sugar
6 tablespoons butter or margarine
½ cup molasses
2 tablespoons milk

Preheat the oven to 325°.

Sift the flour, ginger and soda into a bowl. Stir in the peel and sugar.

Place the butter or margarine, molasses and milk in a saucepan and heat until melted and smooth. Add to the flour mixture and mix to a soft dough.

Break off pieces of the dough and roll into balls about 1–1½ inches in diameter. Place on greased cookie sheets, spacing them well apart, and flatten slightly with the heel of your hand.

Bake for 25–30 minutes or until dark brown around the edges. Cool on a wire rack.

Oatmeal Cookies

MAKES ABOUT 4 DOZEN

¾ cup butter or margarine, softened
⅓ cup honey
1 cup granulated sugar
1 egg
1 teaspoon vanilla
1 cup all-purpose flour
½ teaspoon baking soda
1 teaspoon salt
1 teaspoon cinnamon
2 cups rolled oats
1 cup raisins

Preheat the oven to 350°.

Cream the butter, honey, sugar, egg and vanilla until light and fluffy. Sift the flour, soda, salt and cinnamon into the bowl and stir until blended. Add the rolled oats and raisins and mix well.

Drop by rounded teaspoonfuls onto greased cookie sheets, pressing down to form a patty shape. Leave room between each cookie to allow for spreading.

Bake for 10–12 minutes or until golden brown. Cool on a wire rack.

Date and Nut Cookies

MAKES ABOUT 2½ DOZEN

2 cups all-purpose flour
⅛ teaspoon salt
1 teaspoon baking powder
¼ teaspoon ground allspice
¼ teaspoon ground cardamom
6 tablespoons butter or margarine
⅔ cup firmly packed brown sugar
1 egg
¼ cup milk
⅔ cup finely chopped pitted dates
¼ cup finely chopped filberts
¼ cup finely chopped Brazil nuts

Sift the flour, salt, baking powder, allspice and cardamom into a bowl. Cut in the butter or margarine until the mixture resembles coarse crumbs. Stir in the sugar. Lightly beat the egg with the milk and add to the bowl. Mix well. Mix in the dates, filberts and Brazil nuts. Refrigerate for 30 minutes.

Preheat the oven to 350°.

Roll out the dough on a floured surface to about ¼ inch thick. Cut out 2 inch rounds and place on greased cookie sheets, leaving room for spreading.

Bake for 15 minutes or until golden brown. Cool on a wire rack.

Oaty Coconut Drops

MAKES ABOUT 2 DOZEN

6 tablespoons butter or margarine
1 tablespoon light corn syrup
½ teaspoon baking soda
1 tablespoon boiling water
½ cup all-purpose flour, sifted
⅔ cup rolled oats
⅔ cup shredded coconut
½ cup sugar

Preheat the oven to 325°.

Place the butter or margarine and syrup in a saucepan and heat until melted and smooth. Remove from the heat.

Dissolve the soda in the boiling water and add to the pan. Stir well. Gradually stir in the remaining ingredients.

Drop by rounded teaspoonfuls onto greased cookie sheets, leaving room for spreading. Bake for 20 minutes or until just firm to the touch and golden.

Let cool on the cookie sheets for 5 minutes, then remove to a wire rack to cool completely.

Wasps' Nests

MAKES ABOUT 4 DOZEN

1 cup granulated sugar
¼ cup water
2 cups sliced almonds
3 egg whites
2 cups confectioner's sugar
8 squares (1 oz each) semisweet
　chocolate, grated

Preheat the oven to 300°.

Place the granulated sugar and water in a saucepan and heat, stirring to dissolve the sugar. Bring to a boil and boil, without stirring, until the syrup reaches 230° on a candy thermometer. Remove from the heat and stir in the almonds. Keep warm.

Beat the egg whites until frothy. Gradually beat in the confectioner's sugar and continue beating until the meringue is stiff and glossy. Fold in the almond and syrup mixture and the grated chocolate.

Drop by rounded teaspoonfuls onto greased cookie sheets, leaving room for spreading. Bake for about 25 minutes or until firm to the touch.

Let cool on the cookie sheets for 10 minutes, then remove to a wire rack to cool completely.

Oaty Coconut Drops

Ginger Snaps

MAKES ABOUT 2 DOZEN

6 tablespoons butter or margarine
½ cup sugar
⅓ cup light corn syrup
2 cups self-rising flour
1 teaspoon ground ginger
1 large egg

Preheat the oven to 350°.

Place the butter or margarine, sugar and syrup in a saucepan and heat, stirring, until melted and smooth. Remove from the heat and cool slightly.

Sift the flour and ginger into the saucepan. Add the egg and mix well together.

Drop by rounded teaspoonfuls onto greased cookie sheets, leaving room for spreading. Bake for 15 minutes or until golden.

Let cool on the cookie sheets for 5 minutes, then remove to a wire rack to cool completely.

Cocoa Walnut Drops

MAKES ABOUT 2 DOZEN

1 cup butter or margarine
⅔ cup sugar
¼ teaspoon vanilla
1½ cups all-purpose flour
2 tablespoons unsweetened cocoa
2 cups cornflakes
4 squares (1 oz each) semisweet
** or milk chocolate, melted**
24 walnut halves

Preheat the oven to 350°.

Cream the butter or margarine with the sugar and vanilla until light and fluffy. Sift the flour and cocoa into the bowl and mix well. Fold in the cornflakes.

Drop by rounded teaspoonfuls onto greased cookie sheets, leaving space for spreading. Bake for 15–20 minutes or until just firm to the touch. Let cool on the cookie sheets for 5 minutes, then remove to a wire rack to cool completely.

Drop a blob of melted chocolate on the top of each cookie and press in a walnut half. Let set before serving.

Granola Cookies

MAKES ABOUT 2 DOZEN

4 tablespoons butter or margarine
1 tablespoon light corn syrup
½ teaspoon baking soda
1½ tablespoons boiling water
½ cup all-purpose flour, sifted
½ cup sugar
1 cup granola

Preheat the oven to 300°.

Place the butter or margarine and syrup in a saucepan and heat until melted and smooth. Remove from the heat.

Dissolve the soda in the boiling water and add to the pan. Stir well. Gradually stir in the remaining ingredients.

Drop by rounded teaspoonfuls onto greased cookie sheets, leaving room for spreading. Bake for 20 minutes or until just firm to the touch and golden.

Let cool on the cookie sheets for 5 minutes, then remove to a wire rack to cool completely.

Applesauce Cookies

MAKES ABOUT 4 DOZEN

½ cup butter or margarine
1⅓ cups firmly packed brown sugar
1 egg
2½ cups all-purpose flour
½ teaspoon salt
½ teaspoon baking soda
2 teaspoons apple pie spice
¼ cup apple juice
2 apples, cored and grated
½ cup chopped walnuts
½ cup raisins

Preheat the oven to 375°.

Cream the butter or margarine and sugar together until light and fluffy. Beat in the egg. Sift the flour, salt, soda and spice into the bowl and mix well. Beat in the apple juice. Stir in the apples, walnuts and raisins.

Drop by rounded teaspoonfuls onto greased cookie sheets, leaving room for spreading. Bake for 12–15 minutes or until lightly browned. Cool on a wire rack.

Chocolate Chip Cookies

MAKES ABOUT 4 DOZEN

1 cup butter or margarine
¾ cup granulated sugar
¾ cup firmly packed brown sugar
2 eggs
1 teaspoon vanilla
2¼ cups all-purpose flour
1 teaspoon salt
1 teaspoon baking soda
1 pkg (12 oz) semi sweet chocolate chips
1 cup chopped nuts

Preheat the oven to 375°.

Cream the butter or margarine with the sugars until light and fluffy. Beat in the eggs and vanilla. Sift the flour, salt and soda into the bowl and mix in well. Fold in the chocolate chips and nuts.

Drop the dough by rounded teaspoonfuls onto greased cookie sheets, leaving room for spreading. Bake for 8–10 minutes or until the cookies are lightly browned. Cool on a wire rack.

Chocolate Cinnamon Cookies

MAKES 2 DOZEN

1 cup butter or margarine
½ cup sugar
2 cups self-rising flour
½ teaspoon ground cinnamon
½ cup unsweetened cocoa
1 teaspoon vanilla

Preheat the oven to 350°.

Cream the butter or margarine with the sugar until light and fluffy. Sift the flour, cinnamon and cocoa into the bowl. Add the vanilla and mix to a smooth dough.

Roll teaspoonfuls of the dough into balls and arrange on greased cookie sheets, leaving room for spreading. Dip a fork in cold water and use to flatten the balls.

Bake for 12 minutes or until the cookies are firm. Let cool slightly on the cookie sheets, then remove to a wire rack to cool completely.

If desired, the cookies may be put together in pairs with sweetened whipped cream.

**Chocolate Chip Cookies (left) and
Chocolate Cinnamon Cookies (right).**

Black Pepper Cookies (page 32)

Black Pepper Cookies

MAKES ABOUT 3 DOZEN

¾ cup butter or margarine
¾ teaspoon black pepper
¾ teaspoon ground cinnamon
¼ teaspoon ground cloves
1½ teaspoons vanilla
1 cup sugar
1 egg
1½ cups self-rising flour
¼ teaspoon salt
¾ cup unsweetened cocoa

Preheat the oven to 375°.

Beat the butter or margarine until softened, then beat in the pepper, cinnamon, cloves, vanilla and sugar. Add the egg and beat until the mixture is light and creamy.

Sift the flour, salt and cocoa into the butter mixture and mix to a firm dough. Roll the dough into walnut-size balls with floured hands. Place the balls on greased cookie sheets, spacing them well apart, and flatten with the heel of your hand to about ¼ inch thick.

Bake for 12 minutes or until firm. Cool on a wire rack.

Orange Shortbread

MAKES ABOUT 1 DOZEN

1 cup all-purpose flour
½ cup rice flour
⅛ teaspoon salt
2 tablespoons cream of wheat
grated rind of 1 large orange
5 tablespoons sugar
10 tablespoons butter or margarine
1 tablespoon orange juice or
   brandy

Preheat the oven to 350°.

Sift the flour, rice flour and salt into a bowl and stir in the cream of wheat, orange rind and ¼ cup of the sugar. Cut in the butter or margarine until the mixture resembles fine crumbs. Mix in the orange juice or brandy to make a smooth dough.

Roll the dough into walnut-size balls and place on greased cookie sheets, well spaced apart. Flatten with a fork and sprinkle with the remaining sugar.

Bake for 25–30 minutes or until crisp and golden. Cool on a wire rack.

Forked Sugar Cookies

MAKES ABOUT 2 DOZEN

¾ cup butter or margarine
1¼ cups sugar
2 egg whites, beaten until frothy
1 teaspoon vanilla
2 cups all-purpose flour
2 tablespoons cornstarch

Preheat the oven to 375°.

Cream the butter or margarine with the sugar until light and fluffy. Beat in the egg whites and vanilla. Sift the flour and cornstarch into the bowl and mix well.

With floured hands, roll the dough into walnut-size balls. Place on greased cookie sheets, well spaced apart, and flatten with a fork.

Bake for 15–20 minutes or until golden brown. Cool on a wire rack.

Whole Wheat Shortbread

MAKES 8

1¼ cups whole wheat or graham flour
½ teaspoon salt
⅓ cup firmly packed brown sugar
½ cup butter or margarine
¼ cup granulated sugar

Place the flour in a bowl and stir in the salt and brown sugar. Cut in the butter or margarine until the mixture resembles fine crumbs and knead into a dough.

Press the mixture into a greased 8 inch loose-bottomed fluted cake pan. Score into eight triangles. Refrigerate for 1 hour.

Preheat the oven to 300°.

Bake for 45–60 minutes or until firm to the touch and just beginning to brown.

Sprinkle over half the granulated sugar. Let cool in the pan for 5 minutes, then remove to a wire rack. Sprinkle the other side with the remaining sugar. When cold, break into the triangles.

Almond Chocolate Chip Cookies

MAKES ABOUT 2 DOZEN

½ cup butter or margarine
⅓ cup firmly packed brown sugar
2 cups all-purpose flour, sifted
2 tablespoons light corn syrup
¾ cup chopped almonds
¼ cup semisweet chocolate chips

Preheat the oven to 350°.

Cream the butter or margarine with the sugar until light and fluffy. Beat in the flour and syrup, then mix in the almonds and chocolate chips.

Roll the dough into walnut-size balls and place on greased cookie sheets, spaced well apart. Slightly flatten the balls with a fork.

Bake for 15–20 minutes or until golden brown. Cool on a wire rack.

Spiced Molasses Cookies

MAKES ABOUT 3 DOZEN

2 cups all-purpose flour
½ teaspoon salt
1 teaspoon baking powder
¼ cup sugar
½ teaspoon grated nutmeg
½ teaspoon ground cloves
½ teaspoon ground cinnamon
½ cup molasses
4 tablespoons butter or margarine
¼ cup milk
15 blanched almonds, quartered
   lengthwise

Sift the flour, salt, baking powder, sugar, nutmeg, cloves and cinnamon into a bowl.

Place the molasses and butter or margarine in a heavy-based saucepan and heat until melted and smooth. Stir in the milk, then add to the flour mixture. Mix to a smooth dough. Refrigerate for 1 hour.

Preheat the oven to 375°.

Roll the dough into small walnut-size balls and place on greased cookie sheets. Flatten the balls with the heel of your hand and press an almond quarter into each.

Bake for 12–15 minutes or until just firm to the touch. Cool on a wire rack.

Apricot Urchins

MAKES 6

2 cups all-purpose flour
½ teaspoon salt
¾ cup butter or margarine
¾ cup sugar
2 tablespoons ground almonds
½ cup finely chopped almonds
1 egg white
2 tablespoons apricot jam
1 tablespoon confectioner's sugar

Sift the flour and salt into a bowl. Cut in the butter or margarine until the mixture resembles fine crumbs. Stir in the sugar, ground and chopped almonds and egg white and mix to a soft dough. Refrigerate for 30 minutes.

Preheat the oven to 350°.

Roll out the dough on a floured surface to ¼ inch thick. Cut out twelve 4 inch rounds. Place six of the rounds on a greased cookie sheet. Spread with the jam to within ⅛ inch of the edges.

Using a 2 inch cookie cutter, cut the centers out of the remaining rounds. Place over the jam on the whole rounds and press the edges together. Bake for 10–15 minutes or until golden brown.

Let cool on the cookie sheet for 5 minutes, then remove to a wire rack to cool completely. Sprinkle with the confectioner's sugar before serving.

Apricot Urchins

Filbert Icebox Cookies

MAKES ABOUT 3 DOZEN

4 tablespoons butter or margarine
½ cup sugar
1 egg yolk
¼ teaspoon almond extract (optional)
1 cup self-rising flour, sifted
½ cup chopped toasted filberts

Cream the butter or margarine with the sugar until light and fluffy. Beat in the egg yolk and almond extract, if using it. Add the flour and filberts and mix well.

Shape the dough into a roll about 2 inches in diameter. Wrap in wax paper and refrigerate for 12 hours or overnight.

Preheat the oven to 400°.

Cut the roll of cookie dough into very thin slices and arrange them on greased cookie sheets, leaving room for spreading. Bake for 10–15 minutes or until crisp and lightly browned around the edges. Cool on a wire rack.

Oat Crisps

MAKES ABOUT 2 DOZEN

½ cup butter or margarine
¼ cup sugar
¾ cup all-purpose flour
½ teaspoon salt
¼ teaspoon baking soda
⅓ cup oatmeal

Preheat the oven to 375°.

Cream the butter or margarine with the sugar until light and fluffy. Sift the flour, salt and soda into the bowl and mix well.

With floured hands, roll the dough into walnut-size balls. Coat with the oatmeal. Place on greased cookie sheets, leaving room for spreading.

Bake for 10–15 minutes or until light golden. Cool on a wire rack.

Peanut Butter Cookies

MAKES ABOUT 2 DOZEN

1½ cups all-purpose flour
6 tablespoons butter or margarine
¼ cup crunchy peanut butter
¼ cup water
1 tablespoon sugar

Preheat the oven to 350°.

Sift the flour into a bowl. Cut in the butter or margarine until the mixture resembles fine crumbs. Add the peanut butter and water and mix to a soft dough.

Roll out the dough on a floured surface to a 6×12 inch rectangle. Trim the edges to make them straight, then lift the rectangle onto a greased cookie sheet. Score into 1½×2 inch bars. Sprinkle the sugar over the top.

Bake for 15–20 minutes or until golden brown. Cool on a wire rack, then break into the bars to serve.

Peanut Cookies

MAKES ABOUT 2 DOZEN

2 cups all-purpose flour
1 tablespoon sugar
¼ teaspoon ground allspice
½ cup butter or margarine
3 tablespoons shortening
6–8 tablespoons water
2 tablespoons finely chopped peanuts
¼ cup whole peanuts

Sift the flour, sugar and allspice into a bowl. Cut in the butter or margarine and shortening until the mixture resembles fine crumbs. Mix in enough water to bind to a dough. Work in the chopped peanuts. Refrigerate for 30 minutes.

Preheat the oven to 375°.

Roll out the dough on a floured surface to about ¼ inch thick. Cut out 2 inch rounds and place on greased cookie sheets. Press the whole peanuts into the rounds.

Bake for 15 minutes or until lightly browned at the edges. Let cool on the cookie sheets for 5 minutes, then remove to a wire rack to cool completely.

Funny Faces

MAKES ABOUT 2 DOZEN

1½ cups all-purpose flour
pinch of salt
2 tablespoons hot chocolate powder
½ cup butter or margarine
¼ cup sugar
1 egg
3 tablespoons milk or water
TO DECORATE
1 cup confectioner's sugar
1–2 tablespoons warm water
red food coloring
small candies, raisins, nuts, etc.

Preheat the oven to 325°.

Sift the flour, salt and chocolate powder into a bowl. Cut in the butter or margarine until the mixture resembles fine crumbs. Stir in the sugar. Add the egg and milk or water and mix to a smooth dough.

Roll out the dough on a floured surface to ¼ inch thick. Cut out rounds with a floured 3 inch fluted cookie cutter. Arrange the rounds on greased cookie sheets.

Prick the cookies lightly with a fork, then bake for 10–12 minutes or until lightly browned. Cool on a wire rack.

For the decoration, sift the sugar into a bowl and stir in the water to make a smooth frosting. Tint half the frosting pink with a few drops of food coloring.

Paint features on the cookies using a toothpick dipped in the frosting. Add small candies, raisins, nuts, etc., for eyes, noses, etc., and let set.

Chocolate Peanut Cookies

MAKES ABOUT 1½ DOZEN

4 tablespoons butter or margarine
½ cup firmly packed brown sugar
1 egg
¾ cup self-rising flour
1 tablespoon unsweetened cocoa
2 tablespoons milk
1 cup roughly chopped peanuts

Preheat the oven to 350°.

Cream the butter or margarine with the sugar until light and fluffy. Beat in the egg. Sift the flour and cocoa into the bowl. Add the milk and mix well. Stir in the peanuts.

Drop by rounded teaspoonfuls onto greased cookie sheets, leaving space for spreading. Bake for about 15 minutes or until firm to the touch. Let cool on the cookie sheets for 5 minutes, then remove to a wire rack to cool completely.

Funny Faces

Sour Cream Nutmeg Cookies

MAKES ABOUT 3 DOZEN

4 tablespoons butter or margarine
1½ cups sugar
2 eggs
2½ cups all-purpose flour
¼ teaspoon salt
1 teaspoon baking soda
1 teaspoon grated nutmeg
1 cup sour cream

Preheat the oven to 375°.

Cream the butter or margarine with the sugar until light and fluffy. Beat in the eggs. Sift the flour, salt, soda and nutmeg into the bowl. Add the sour cream and mix well.

Drop by tablespoonfuls onto greased cookie sheets, leaving room for spreading. Bake for 12–15 minutes or until just firm to the touch and golden brown. Cool on a wire rack.

Chocolate Oat Cookies

MAKES ABOUT 1 DOZEN

1 cup self-rising flour
½ teaspoon salt
1 tablespoon unsweetened cocoa
½ cup butter or margarine
½ cup sugar
¾ cup rolled oats
¼ cup strong black coffee

Preheat the oven to 350°.

Sift the flour, salt and cocoa into a bowl. Cut in the butter or margarine until the mixture resembles fine crumbs. Stir in the sugar and all but 2 tablespoons of the oats. Add the coffee and mix to a soft dough.

Roll the dough into walnut-size balls and coat with the remaining oats. Place on greased cookie sheets, spaced well apart, and flatten with the heel of your hand to about ¼ inch thick.

Bake for 15 minutes or until crisp and golden. Cool on a wire rack.

Orange and Lemon Cookies

MAKES ABOUT 4 DOZEN

2¾ cups all-purpose flour
2½ teaspoons baking powder
¼ teaspoon salt
⅔ cup granulated sugar
½ cup firmly packed dark brown sugar
1 teaspoon grated lemon rind
2 teaspoons grated orange rind
10 tablespoons butter or margarine
2 eggs
¼ cup light cream

Preheat the oven to 350°.

Sift the flour, baking powder, salt and sugars into a bowl. Stir in the lemon and orange rinds. Cut in the butter or margarine until the mixture resembles coarse crumbs.

Lightly beat the eggs with the cream. Add to the bowl and mix to a soft dough. Drop by rounded teaspoonfuls onto greased cookie sheets, leaving room for spreading.

Bake for 15–20 minutes or until lightly browned. Cool on a wire rack.

Coconut Cornflake Kisses

MAKES ABOUT 4 DOZEN

3 egg whites
½ teaspoon cream of tartar
1 cup sugar
1 teaspoon vanilla
¾ cup shredded coconut
1 cup cornflakes

Preheat the oven to 300°.

Beat the egg whites with the cream of tartar until fluffy. Gradually beat in the sugar and vanilla and continue beating until the mixture is stiff and glossy. Fold in the coconut and cornflakes.

Drop by rounded teaspoonfuls onto greased and floured cookie sheets, leaving space for spreading. Bake for about 20 minutes or until set and lightly colored.

Let cool on the cookie sheets for 5 minutes, then remove to a wire rack to cool completely.

Gingerbread People

MAKES ABOUT 3½ DOZEN

¾ cup butter or margarine
½ cup firmly packed brown sugar
⅔ cup molasses
⅓ cup dark corn syrup
5 cups all-purpose flour
3 teaspoons ground ginger
1½ teaspoons ground allspice
1½ teaspoons baking soda
2 eggs

Place the butter or margarine, sugar, molasses and syrup in a saucepan and heat until melted and smooth. Remove from the heat.

Sift the flour, spices and soda into a bowl. Add the eggs and the melted mixture and mix to a smooth dough. Refrigerate for 2 hours.

Preheat the oven to 350°.

Roll out the dough on a floured surface to ¼ inch thick. Cut out people with a small floured gingerbread cookie cutter, or cut them out freehand with a sharp knife. Arrange on greased cookie sheets, leaving room for spreading.

Bake for 15–20 minutes or until firm to the touch. Cool on a wire rack.

Paint on faces and clothing with confectioner's sugar frosting (see photograph and Funny Faces, page 39).

Rainbow Pinwheels

MAKES ABOUT 1½ DOZEN

½ cup butter or margarine
½ cup sugar
1 egg
2 cups all-purpose flour
2 teaspoons baking powder
½ teaspoon salt
1 tablespoon instant coffee powder
1 tablespoon hot water
½ teaspoon vanilla
1 tablespoon grated orange rind
green food coloring
2 tablespoons chopped candied angelica

Cream the butter or margarine with the sugar until light and fluffy. Beat in the egg. Sift the flour, baking powder and salt into the bowl and mix to a smooth dough.

Divide the dough into three equal portions. Dissolve the instant coffee in the hot water and add to one portion of dough. Mix until evenly combined. Add the vanilla and orange rind to the second portion of dough and mix until evenly combined. Add enough food coloring to the third portion of dough to tint it pale green. Work in the angelica. Wrap the three portions of dough in plastic wrap and refrigerate for 1 hour.

Roll out each portion of dough into a 9×6 inch rectangle. Place the orange rectangle on the coffee rectangle and the green rectangle on the top. Starting from a short side, roll up like a jelly roll.

(At this stage, the roll may be refrigerated for up to 1 week. Remove it from the refrigerator 15 minutes before baking.)

Preheat the oven to 400°.

Cut the roll into ¼ inch thick slices and arrange them on greased cookie sheets, leaving room for spreading. Bake for 8–10 minutes or until just firm to the touch. Let cool on the cookie sheets for 5 minutes, then remove to a wire rack to cool.

Gingerbread People

Rainbow Pinwheels

Mincemeat Drops

MAKES ABOUT 3 DOZEN

½ cup butter or margarine
1 cup sugar
½ teaspoon grated orange rind
2 eggs
2½ cups all-purpose flour
2 teaspoons baking powder
½ teaspoon salt
1 cup mincemeat

Preheat the oven to 375°.
Cream the butter or margarine with the sugar and orange rind until light and fluffy. Beat in the eggs. Sift the flour, baking powder and salt into the bowl. Add the mincemeat and mix well together.
Drop by rounded teaspoonfuls onto greased cookie sheets, leaving room for spreading. Bake for 10–12 minutes or until the edges are lightly browned. Cool on a wire rack.

Sugar Cookies

MAKES ABOUT 3½ DOZEN

½ cup butter or margarine
1¼ cups sugar
1 egg
1 teaspoon vanilla
1 tablespoon light cream
2 cups all-purpose flour
½ teaspoon salt
1 teaspoon baking powder

Cream the butter or margarine with 1 cup of the sugar until light and fluffy. Beat in the egg, vanilla and cream. Sift the flour, salt and baking powder into the bowl and mix well. Refrigerate overnight.
Preheat the oven to 375°.
Roll out the dough on a floured surface to about ⅛ inch thick. Cut out 3 inch rounds, using a floured plain or fluted cookie cutter, or cut out other shapes. Arrange on greased cookie sheets and sprinkle over the remaining sugar.
Bake for about 5–8 minutes or until just firm to the touch and lightly golden. Cool on a wire rack.

No-Bake Chocolate Munchies

MAKES 10

4 tablespoons butter or margarine
2 tablespoons honey
¼ cup sugar
2 tablespoons unsweetened cocoa
1 cup puffed rice cereal
1 tablespoon raisins

Place the butter or margarine, honey and sugar in a saucepan and heat over low heat, stirring until the butter has melted and the sugar dissolved. Remove from the heat and stir in the cocoa until evenly combined.

Add the cereal and raisins and mix together well. Divide the mixture evenly among 10 small paper baking cups and chill until set.

Lemon Cookies

MAKES ABOUT 1 DOZEN

½ cup butter or margarine
½ cup sugar
1 egg yolk
2 cups all-purpose flour, sifted
2 teaspoons grated lemon rind

Preheat the oven to 350°.

Cream the butter or margarine with the sugar until light and fluffy. Beat in the egg yolk. Add the flour and lemon rind and mix to a smooth dough. Refrigerate for 10 minutes.

Roll out the dough on a floured surface to ¼ inch thick. Cut out 4 inch rounds and place on cookie sheets. Bake for 12–15 minutes or until golden brown around the edges. Cool on a wire rack.

Cocoa Fork Cookies

MAKES ABOUT 2½ DOZEN

½ cup butter or margarine
½ cup sugar
1¼ cups self-rising flour
pinch of salt
3 tablespoons unsweetened cocoa
3 tablespoons milk or water

Preheat the oven to 375°.

Cream the butter or margarine with the sugar until light and fluffy. Sift the flour, salt and cocoa into the bowl and mix well. Add the milk or water and mix to a soft dough.

Roll the dough into walnut-size balls and arrange on greased cookie sheets, spaced well apart. Flatten the balls slightly with a fork.

Bake for 8 minutes or until just firm to the touch. Cool on a wire rack.

Easter Bunnies

MAKES 10

6 tablespoons butter or margarine
¼ cup + 1 tablespoon sugar
1 egg, separated
1½ cups all-purpose flour
1½ teaspoons baking powder
¼ teaspoon salt
¼ cup warm milk

Cream the butter or margarine with ¼ cup of the sugar until light and fluffy. Beat in the egg yolk. Sift the flour, baking powder and salt into the bowl. Add the milk and mix to a soft dough. Cover and refrigerate for 1 hour or until the dough is firm.

Preheat the oven to 400°.

Roll out the dough on a floured surface to about ¼ inch thick. Using floured round cookie cutters, cut out ten 2 inch rounds, ten 1 inch rounds, twenty ¾ inch rounds, and ten ½ inch rounds. Make up the bunnies using the largest rounds for the body, the medium-size rounds for the head and the smallest rounds for the tail. To make the ears, flatten the ¾ inch rounds and shape into ovals.

Place the bunnies on greased cookie sheets. Bake for 10 minutes.

Beat the egg white until frothy. Brush over the bunnies and sprinkle with the remaining sugar. Return to the oven and bake for 10 minutes longer or until golden and firm. Cool on the cookie sheets.

If desired, the bunnies may be decorated with small candies, and children's names piped on in colored frosting.

Easter Bunnies

Chapter Three

BARS AND FILLED COOKIES

Sesame and Honey Slices

MAKES 8–10

½ cup honey
3 tablespoons chopped toasted filberts
2 tablespoons sesame seeds
½ cup butter or margarine
1 cup whole wheat flour
1 teaspoon baking powder
1 teaspoon ground cinnamon
2 eggs, beaten

Preheat the oven to 350°.

Place 3 tablespoons of the honey in a greased 12×8 inch baking pan and spread it out evenly. Scatter over the filberts and sesame seeds.

Cream the butter or margarine with the remaining honey until fluffy. Beat in the flour, baking powder, cinnamon and eggs. Pour the batter into the pan and spread it out.

Bake for 25 minutes. Let cool in the pan, then cut into neat slices.

Fudge Butter Bars

MAKES ABOUT 32

1 cup self-rising flour
pinch of salt
6 tablespoons butter or margarine
6 tablespoons sugar
1 egg, beaten
⅛ teaspoon vanilla
TOPPING
4 tablespoons butter or margarine
⅓ cup firmly packed brown sugar
1¾ cups sweetened condensed milk
6 squares (1 oz each) semisweet
   chocolate

Preheat the oven to 375°.

Sift the flour and salt into a bowl. Cut in the butter or margarine until the mixture resembles coarse bread crumbs. Stir in the sugar, then add the egg and vanilla and mix to a smooth dough.

Press the dough into a greased 12 × 8 inch baking pan. Bake for about 10–15 minutes or until golden brown. Let cool in the pan.

To make the topping, place the butter or margarine and sugar in a saucepan and heat gently, stirring to melt the butter and dissolve the sugar. Add the condensed milk and bring to a boil. Boil, stirring, until the mixture reaches 240° on a candy thermometer (soft ball stage). Stir in 2 squares (2 oz) of the chocolate until melted, then remove from the heat and beat until the mixture cools and thickens. Pour over the cookie base in the pan and let cool.

Melt the remaining chocolate over low heat. Pour over the fudge topping and tap the pan on the countertop to level the chocolate. Chill for about 1 hour or until set, then cut into bars to serve.

Granola Bars

MAKES ABOUT 16

1 pkg (12 oz) granola cereal
¼ cup honey
¼ cup light corn syrup
¼ cup vegetable oil
1 teaspoon ground cinnamon

Preheat the oven to 350°.

Mix together all the ingredients, then press into a greased 11 × 7 inch baking pan. Bake for 15 minutes.

Let cool for 5 minutes, then cut into bars. Cool completely in the pan.

Cherry Diamonds

MAKES 18–20

3 eggs
½ cup sugar
½ teaspoon vanilla
6 tablespoons butter or margarine,
    melted
1 cup self-rising flour, sifted
FILLING
½ cup finely chopped canned pitted
    cherries
2 tablespoons confectioner's sugar
2 tablespoons ground almonds
FROSTING
5 tablespoons confectioner's sugar
5 teaspoons hot water
1 drop red food coloring
DECORATION
candied angelica leaves
halved candied cherries

Preheat the oven to 350°

Beat the eggs, sugar and vanilla until very thick and pale. Fold in the butter or margarine and flour. Pour into a greased 11×7 inch baking pan and spread out evenly.

Bake for 25 minutes or until a wooden toothpick inserted into the center of the mixture comes out clean. Invert onto a wire rack and let cool. Cut crosswise into two equal pieces.

Mix together the filling ingredients. Spread over one layer and place the other layer on top.

To make the frosting, sift the sugar into a small bowl and stir in the water and food coloring. Pour the frosting over the top of the cake and spread it to the edges. Cut into 1½ inch wide strips, then cut the strips diagonally into 1½ inch diamond shapes.

Decorate each diamond with angelica leaves and half a cherry and let set before serving.

Fruity Lemon Fingers

MAKES ABOUT 18

½ cup butter or margarine
½ cup sugar
1 egg, beaten
2 cups self-rising flour, sifted
pinch of salt
1 cup mixed dried fruit (raisins,
    golden raisins, currants)
TOPPING
1 tablespoon butter or margarine,
    melted
1 tablespoon boiling water
1 teaspoon grated lemon rind
1 tablespoon lemon juice
1½ cups confectioner's sugar, sifted
½ cup sliced almonds

Preheat the oven to 350°.

Place the butter or margarine in a saucepan and melt over low heat. Stir in the sugar until dissolved, then remove from the heat. Add the egg, flour, salt and dried fruit and mix well.

Pour the mixture into a greased 12×8 inch baking pan and spread out evenly. Bake for 20–25 minutes. Cool on a wire rack.

To make the topping, mix together the butter or margarine, water and lemon rind and juice. Gradually beat in the sugar. Pour over the cookie base and smooth the surface. Sprinkle with the almonds and let set. Cut into fingers to serve.

Fruity Lemon Fingers

Honey Walnut Bars

½ cup sugar
½ cup honey
¼ cup water
½ cup semisweet chocolate chips
1 cup chopped walnuts
2 cups all-purpose flour
1 teaspoon baking powder
1 teaspoon baking soda
½ teaspoon ground cinnamon
2 eggs

Preheat the oven to 350°.

Place the sugar, honey and water in a saucepan and heat gently, stirring to dissolve the sugar. Bring to a boil, then remove from the heat. Stir in the chocolate chips and walnuts and continue stirring until the chocolate has melted. Let cool.

Sift the flour, baking powder, soda and cinnamon into a bowl. Beat in the eggs and honey mixture. Pour into a greased 13×9 inch baking pan.

Bake for 35 minutes. Cut into small bars, then let cool in the pan.

Chocolate-Covered Pecan Crunchies

4 tablespoons butter or margarine
¼ cup light corn syrup
⅓ cup firmly packed brown sugar
3 tablespoons unsweetened cocoa
1 egg
1 teaspoon vanilla
2 cups shortbread cookie crumbs
1 cup shredded coconut
½ cup chopped pecans
4 squares (1 oz each) semisweet
  chocolate, melted
FILLING
6 tablespoons butter or margarine
3 cups confectioner's sugar, sifted
1 egg, beaten

Place the butter or margarine, syrup, sugar, cocoa, egg and vanilla in a saucepan. Cook over low heat, stirring, until the mixture is smooth. Remove from the heat and stir in the shortbread crumbs, coconut and pecans.

Press the pecan mixture over the bottom of a greased 9 inch square baking pan. Chill until set.

To make the filling, cream the butter or margarine until softened, then gradually beat in the confectioner's sugar alternately with the egg. Spread the filling over the cookie base and chill for 30 minutes longer.

Spread the melted chocolate over the filling and chill until set. Cut into squares to serve.

Crunchy Marmalade Bars

MAKES ABOUT 15

1⅓ cups rolled oats
1¼ cups all-purpose flour, sifted
½ cup firmly packed brown sugar
½ teaspoon ground allspice
½ teaspoon ground cardamom
¾ cup butter or margarine
6 tablespoons marmalade

Preheat the oven to 350°.

Mix together the oats, flour, sugar and spices. Cut in the butter or margarine until the mixture resembles coarse bread crumbs.

Press half the oat mixture over the bottom of a greased 8 inch square baking pan. Spread the marmalade over and cover with the remaining oat mixture. Press down lightly.

Bake for 35–40 minutes or until lightly browned. Cut into bars, then let cool in the pan.

Dried Apricot Bars

MAKES ABOUT 15

¾ cup dried apricots, soaked overnight
½ cup butter or margarine
¼ cup granulated sugar
1½ cups all-purpose flour, sifted
½ teaspoon baking powder
¼ teaspoon salt
2 eggs
1⅓ cups firmly packed brown sugar
½ teaspoon vanilla
½ cup finely chopped walnuts
½ cup confectioner's sugar

Preheat the oven to 350°.

Drain the apricots and finely chop them. Set aside.

Cream the butter or margarine and granulated sugar together until light and fluffy. Add 1 cup of the flour and cut together until the mixture resembles fine bread crumbs. Press the mixture over the bottom of a greased 8 inch square baking pan. Bake for 25 minutes or until lightly browned.

Meanwhile, sift the remaining flour into a bowl with the baking powder and salt. Lightly beat the eggs with the brown sugar, then add to the flour and combine well. Stir in the vanilla, walnuts and apricots.

Spread the apricot mixture over the cookie base in the pan and return to the oven. Bake for 30 minutes longer.

Let cool in the pan, then cut into ½ × 1 inch bars. Coat with the confectioner's sugar.

Flapjacks

MAKES 9

6 tablespoons butter or margarine
2 tablespoons brown sugar
⅛ teaspoon salt
¼ teaspoon ground ginger
3 tablespoons light corn syrup
1 tablespoon honey
1½ cups rolled oats
9 blanched almonds

Preheat the oven to 375°.

Beat the butter or margarine with the sugar, salt, ginger, syrup and honey until light and fluffy. Mix in the oats. Press the mixture into a greased 8 inch square baking pan and smooth the surface. Score lightly into nine squares and press an almond into the center of each.

Bake for 25 minutes or until lightly browned and firm to the touch. Cut into squares along the marked lines, then let cool in the pan.

Flapjacks

Brownies

MAKES ABOUT 16

**2 squares (1 oz each) unsweetened
  chocolate
4 tablespoons butter or margarine
1 cup sugar
2 eggs, beaten
1 teaspoon vanilla
⅔ cup all-purpose flour
½ teaspoon baking powder
¼ teaspoon salt
½ cup chopped walnuts**

Preheat the oven to 350°.

Place the chocolate and butter or margarine in a saucepan and heat gently until melted and smooth. Remove from the heat and stir in the sugar until dissolved. Add the eggs and vanilla and mix well.

Sift the flour with the baking powder and salt and beat into the chocolate mixture. Fold in the walnuts.

Pour the batter into a greased 8 inch square baking pan. Bake for 25 minutes or until a wooden toothpick inserted into the center comes out clean. Cool in the pan, then cut into 2 inch squares to serve.

Brownies

Date Bars

MAKES ABOUT 12

½ lb pitted dates (about 1½ cups)
¾ cup water
2 tablespoons honey
½ teaspoon ground allspice
1¼ cups whole wheat flour
1 cup rolled oats
1 cup butter or margarine

Place the dates and water in a saucepan and bring to a boil. Simmer for 15–20 minutes or until the dates are soft. Remove from the heat and mash the dates until smooth. Mix in the honey and allspice. Let cool.

Preheat the oven to 350°.

Place the flour and oats in a bowl. Cut in the butter or margarine until the mixture resembles coarse bread crumbs.

Press half the oat mixture over the bottom of a greased 8 inch square baking pan. Spread over the date mixture, then cover with the remaining oat mixture and press down firmly.

Bake for 25–30 minutes or until golden brown. Cut into bars, then let cool in the pan.

Jam and Coconut Bars

MAKES ABOUT 12

½ cup butter or margarine
½ cup sugar
2 eggs, beaten
2 cups all-purpose flour
1 teaspoon baking powder
¼ teaspoon salt
½ cup shredded coconut
¾ cup raspberry or strawberry jam

Preheat the oven to 400°.

Cream the butter or margarine with the sugar until light and fluffy. Beat in the eggs. Sift the flour with the baking powder and salt and mix into the butter mixture with the coconut.

Spread half the coconut batter over the bottom of a greased 8 inch square baking pan. Spread the jam over, then cover with the remaining coconut batter.

Bake for 25 minutes or until the top is lightly browned and will spring back when lightly pressed.

Let cool in the pan before cutting into bars.

So'mores

MAKES 20

20 graham crackers
12 squares (1 oz each) semisweet
  chocolate, melted
2 cups chopped walnuts
½ lb marshmallows

Spread out the graham crackers on cookie sheets or wax paper. Spread over the melted chocolate and scatter the walnuts on top. Let set.

Melt the marshmallows over low heat. Spread the melted marshmallows generously over the graham crackers and let cool until set. Serve fresh.

Coffee Pecan Bars

MAKES ABOUT 25

½ cup butter or margarine
1 cup sugar
1 egg
1½ cups all-purpose flour, sifted
5–6 tablespoons strong black coffee
2 cups chopped pecans
3 egg whites

Preheat the oven to 350°.

Cream the butter or margarine with ¼ cup of the sugar until light and fluffy. Beat in the egg, then work in the flour alternately with the coffee, to make a smooth dough.

Press the dough over the bottom of a greased 8 inch square baking pan. Bake for 15 minutes.

Meanwhile, place the pecans, egg whites and remaining sugar in a saucepan. Heat gently, stirring to dissolve the sugar, then bring to a boil and cook, stirring frequently, for 6–8 minutes or until the mixture pulls away from the sides of the pan.

Spread the pecan mixture over the cookie base in the pan. Return to the oven and bake for 15 minutes longer. Let cool in the pan, then cut into bars.

Date and Walnut Diamonds

MAKES ABOUT 15

½ cup butter or margarine
½ cup sugar
2 egg yolks
½ teaspoon vanilla
2 cups self-rising flour, sifted
TOPPING
3 tablespoons apricot jam
2 teaspoons lemon juice
2 egg whites
1 tablespoon sugar
⅓ cup finely chopped pitted dates
½ cup finely chopped walnuts
1 teaspoon grated orange rind

Preheat the oven to 350°.

Cream the butter or margarine with the sugar until light and fluffy. Beat in the egg yolks and vanilla, then mix in the flour. Pour the mixture into a greased 8 inch square baking pan and press evenly into the corners. Prick all over with a fork.

Bake for 10 minutes or until the edges are golden brown.

Meanwhile, mix the jam with the lemon juice.

Remove the pan from the oven and spread the jam mixture over the cookie base.

Beat the egg whites until frothy. Add the sugar and continue beating until stiff. Fold in the dates, walnuts and orange rind. Spread over the jam-glazed cookie base.

Return the pan to the oven and bake for 15 minutes longer or until the topping is golden brown and just firm to the touch. Let cool in the pan for 20 minutes, then cut into diamond shapes.

Honey Oat Fingers

MAKES 16

2 tablespoons honey
2 tablespoons light corn syrup
6 tablespoons butter or margarine
⅔ cup firmly packed brown sugar
2 cups rolled oats

Preheat the oven to 350°.

Put the honey, syrup, butter or margarine and sugar into a saucepan and heat gently, stirring, until melted. Remove from the heat and stir in the oats. Pour the mixture into a greased 8 inch square baking pan.

Bake for 20–30 minutes or until golden brown. Cut into 4×1 inch fingers while still warm, then let cool in the pan.

Mallow Brownies

MAKES ABOUT 16

6 tablespoons butter or margarine
1 cup firmly packed brown sugar
2 egg yolks, beaten
1 teaspoon vanilla
¾ cup all-purpose flour
1 teaspoon baking powder
¼ teaspoon salt
½ cup chopped walnuts
20 large marshmallows
TOPPING
4 tablespoons butter or margarine
1½ cups firmly packed brown sugar
¼ teaspoon salt
⅓ cup light cream
1 teaspoon vanilla

Preheat the oven to 350°.

Cream the butter or margarine with the sugar until light and fluffy. Beat in the egg yolks and vanilla. Sift the flour with the baking powder and salt, then beat into the butter mixture. Fold in the walnuts.

Pour the batter into a greased 8 inch square baking pan. Bake for 30 minutes or until a wooden toothpick inserted into the center comes out clean. Let cool in the pan.

Melt the marshmallows over low heat. Pour over the top of the brownie base in the pan.

To make the topping, place the butter or margarine, sugar, salt and cream in a saucepan and bring to a boil, stirring to dissolve the sugar. Boil until the mixture reaches 240° on a candy thermometer (soft ball stage). Remove from the heat and let cool, without stirring, for 4 minutes. Add the vanilla and beat until the mixture is thick and creamy.

Pour the topping evenly over the melted marshmallow. Let cool until set, then cut into squares.

Mallow Brownies

Prune Bars

MAKES ABOUT 20

3 eggs
1 cup sugar
1 cup self-rising flour, sifted
¼ teaspoon grated nutmeg
¼ teaspoon ground allspice
1 teaspoon vanilla
1¾ cups chopped pitted prunes
confectioner's sugar to dredge

Preheat the oven to 325°.

Beat the eggs and sugar together until very thick and pale. Add the flour, spices and vanilla and beat until well combined. Fold in the prunes.

Pour the batter into a greased and floured 12×8 inch baking pan. Bake for 25–30 minutes or until golden brown. Let cool in the pan, then cut into bars and dredge with confectioner's sugar.

No-Bake Mocha Orange Bars

MAKES ABOUT 25

½ cup butter or margarine
½ cup sugar
1 egg, beaten
1 teaspoon grated orange rind
2 tablespoons unsweetened cocoa
1 cup chopped walnuts
2 cups plain sweet cookie crumbs
   (e.g., sugar cookies, vanilla wafers, etc.)
TOPPING
2 squares (1 oz each) semisweet chocolate
4 tablespoons butter or margarine
3 tablespoons strong black coffee
1 teaspoon vanilla
2½ cups confectioner's sugar, sifted
½ cup chopped walnuts

Place the butter or margarine in a saucepan and melt over low heat. Stir in the sugar until dissolved, then bring to a boil. Remove from the heat and let cool slightly, then add the egg, orange rind, cocoa, nuts and cookie crumbs. Mix well.

Press the mixture into a greased 8 inch square baking pan. Chill while making the topping.

Place the chocolate and butter or margarine in a heavy-based saucepan and melt over low heat. Stir in the coffee and vanilla. Remove from the heat and gradually beat in the sugar. If the frosting is too thick to spread, add a little hot water.

Spread the frosting over the cookie base. Sprinkle with the nuts. Let set, then cut into bars to serve.

Fruit and Nut Squares

MAKES 24

2 cups shortbread cookie crumbs
6 tablespoons butter or margarine, melted
⅓ cup firmly packed brown sugar
⅔ cup raisins
1 cup halved candied cherries
⅔ cup chopped walnuts
1 cup sweetened condensed milk

Mix the cookie crumbs with the butter or margarine and sugar, then press over the bottom of a greased 9 inch square baking pan. Chill for 30 minutes.

Scatter the raisins, cherries and walnuts over the cookie base. Pour the condensed milk over and let soak for 30 minutes.

Preheat the oven to 325°.

Bake for 10–15 minutes or until all visible milk has set. Let cool in the pan, then cut into 1½ inch squares.

Applejacks

MAKES ABOUT 18

6 tablespoons butter or margarine
⅓ cup firmly packed brown sugar
6 tablespoons light corn syrup
2¼ cups rolled oats
⅛ teaspoon salt
TOPPING
3 tablespoons apricot jam
2 teaspoons orange juice
2 apples, peeled, cored and thinly sliced
1 tablespoon butter or margarine
½ teaspoon ground cinnamon

Preheat the oven to 350°.

Place the butter or margarine, sugar and syrup in a saucepan and heat gently, stirring until the butter has melted and the sugar dissolved. Remove from the heat and gradually stir in the oats and salt. Press the mixture into a greased 9 inch square baking pan.

Strain the jam into a small saucepan and add the orange juice. Stir over low heat until runny. Spread about half the jam glaze over the oat base in the pan. Arrange the apple slices on top, in three separate rows lengthwise, slightly overlapping the slices.

Add the butter or margarine and cinnamon to the remaining jam glaze and heat until the butter has melted. Brush this glaze over the apple slices.

Bake for 30–35 minutes or until the apples are tender and the flapjack base is golden brown. Cut into bars, then let cool in the pan.

Butterscotch Brownies

MAKES ABOUT 16

½ cup butter or margarine, melted
1 cup firmly packed brown sugar
2 eggs, beaten
1 cup self-rising flour, sifted
⅛ teaspoon salt
1 teaspoon vanilla
½ cup chopped pecans

Preheat the oven to 350°.

Put all the ingredients into a bowl and mix well. Pour into a greased 8 inch square baking pan.

Bake for 25 minutes or until a wooden toothpick inserted into the center comes out clean. Cut into squares while still warm, then let cool in the pan.

Cherry Marshmallow Squares

MAKES ABOUT 16

¾ cup butter or margarine
⅓ cup sugar
½ teaspoon vanilla
1½ cups all-purpose flour, sifted
24 large marshmallows
6 tablespoons milk
½ cup chopped almonds
½ cup chopped candied cherries

Preheat the oven to 325°.

Cream the butter or margarine with the sugar until light and fluffy. Beat in the vanilla, then work in the flour to make a smooth dough.

Press the dough over the bottom of a greased 8 inch square baking pan. Bake for 20–25 minutes or until golden brown. Let cool in the pan.

Place the marshmallows and milk in a saucepan and heat gently to melt the marshmallows. Fold in the almonds and cherries. Let cool slightly, then spread over the cookie base in the pan.

Cool until the marshmallow topping has set. Cut into 2 inch squares to serve.

Cherry Marshmallow Squares (left),
Marshmallows coated with confectioner's
sugar and with coconut (page 126).

No-Bake Fudge Fingers

MAKES ABOUT 22

½ cup butter or margarine
1 cup firmly packed brown sugar
¼ cup heavy cream
2 squares (1 oz each) semisweet
   chocolate
1 cup chopped walnuts
½ cup chopped toasted filberts
2 cups graham cracker crumbs

Place the butter or margarine, sugar, cream and chocolate in a saucepan and heat gently, stirring to melt the chocolate and butter. Remove from the heat and stir in the walnuts, filberts and crumbs.

Pour into a greased 12×8 inch baking pan and spread out evenly. Chill for at least 1 hour before cutting into fingers.

Chocolate Orange Fingers

MAKES ABOUT 18

½ cup butter or margarine
grated rind of 1 orange
¼ cup confectioner's sugar, sifted
1 cup all-purpose flour, sifted
TOPPING
¼ cup confectioner's sugar, sifted
1 tablespoon orange juice
2 tablespoons apricot jam, warmed
4 squares (1 oz each) semisweet
   chocolate, melted

Cream the butter or margarine with the orange rind until softened, then gradually beat in the sugar. Work in the flour.

Put the dough into a cookie press. Using the star plate, form long strips of dough on greased cookie sheets. Cut into 3½ inch lengths. Chill for 1 hour.

Preheat the oven to 325°.

Bake for 15–20 minutes or until golden brown.

Meanwhile, for the topping, mix together the confectioner's sugar and orange juice until smooth.

Brush the tops of the cookies with the jam, then cover with the orange frosting. Return to the oven and bake for 5 minutes longer. Cool on a wire rack.

Dip the ends of the cookies into the melted chocolate and let set on wax paper.

Viennese Fingers

MAKES ABOUT 12

1 cup butter or margarine
½ cup confectioner's sugar, sifted
2 cups all-purpose flour, sifted
2 teaspoons grated orange rind
1 tablespoon orange juice
6 squares (1 oz each) semisweet
   chocolate, melted
FILLING
4 tablespoons butter or margarine
1 cup confectioner's sugar, sifted
⅛ teaspoon vanilla

Preheat the oven to 350°.

Cream the butter or margarine with the sugar until light and fluffy. Beat in the flour and orange rind and juice until smooth.

Put the dough into a cookie press. Using the star plate, form long strips of dough on greased cookie sheets. Cut into 3 inch lengths. Bake for 10–15 minutes or until pale golden and firm to the touch. Cool on the cookie sheets for 5 minutes, then remove to a wire rack to cool completely.

To make the filling, cream the butter or margarine until soft. Gradually beat in the sugar followed by the vanilla.

Put the cookies together in pairs with the filling. Dip each end of the cookies in the melted chocolate and let dry on wax paper.

Chocolate Pineapple Rings

MAKES 10

10 tablespoons butter or margarine
¼ cup sugar
1½ cups all-purpose flour, sifted
3 tablespoons ground almonds
¼ teaspoon almond extract
8 squares (1 oz each) semisweet
   chocolate
10 canned pineapple rings
10 maraschino cherries
1 teaspoon cornstarch
¼ cup pineapple syrup (from the can)

Preheat the oven to 375°.

Cream ½ cup of the butter or margarine with the sugar until light and fluffy. Add the flour, ground almonds and almond extract and mix to a soft dough.

Roll out the dough thinly. Cut into 20 3 inch rounds and arrange on greased cookie sheets. Prick the rounds with a fork. Bake for 20 minutes or until lightly browned. Cool on a wire rack.

Melt the chocolate with the remaining butter or margarine in a heavy-based saucepan. Let cool slightly, then spread the chocolate over the cookies. Place the cookies together in pairs before the chocolate sets, arranging each pair so there is chocolate between and chocolate on top. Place a pineapple ring on each cookie pair and put a cherry in the center. Let set.

Dissolve the cornstarch in the pineapple syrup in a small saucepan. Bring to a boil, stirring, and cook until thickened. Let cool to room temperature, then brush the glaze over the pineapple rings. Let set.

Chocolate Mint Cookies

MAKES ABOUT 2 DOZEN

⅔ cup butter or margarine
1 cup sugar
1 egg, lightly beaten
2 cups all-purpose flour
1 teaspoon baking powder
½ teaspoon baking soda
½ teaspoon salt
¾ cup unsweetened cocoa
¼ cup milk
FILLING
2 cups confectioner's sugar
⅛ teaspoon salt
3 tablespoons light cream
¼ teaspoon mint flavoring
few drops of green food coloring

Cream the butter or margarine with the sugar until light and fluffy. Beat in the egg. Sift the flour, baking powder, soda, salt and cocoa into the bowl. Add the milk and mix to a soft dough.

Form the dough into a roll about 2 inches in diameter. Wrap in wax paper and refrigerate overnight.

Preheat the oven to 325°.

Cut the roll of dough into ⅛ inch thick slices and arrange on ungreased cookie sheets. Bake for 10–12 minutes or until firm to the touch. Cool on a wire rack.

To make the filling, mix the sugar with the salt, then gradually stir in the cream until smooth. Add the mint flavoring and food coloring.

Put the cookies together in pairs with the filling.

Coconut Squares

MAKES 16

½ cup butter or margarine
1 tablespoon honey
½ cup firmly packed brown sugar
¾ cup shredded coconut
1 cup rolled oats
6 tablespoons lightly crushed cornflakes

Preheat the oven to 325°.

Place the butter or margarine and honey in a saucepan and heat gently until the butter has melted. Remove from the heat and stir in the remaining ingredients. Pour into a greased 8 inch square baking pan and spread out evenly.

Bake for 30 minutes or until golden brown. Cut into squares and let cool in the pan.

Coconut Squares

Ladyfinger Cookies

MAKES ABOUT 20

4 eggs, separated
½ cup sugar
⅛ teaspoon almond extract
¾ cup all-purpose flour, sifted
sugar for dredging

Preheat the oven to 350°.

Place the egg yolks, sugar and almond extract in a bowl and beat until very thick and pale. Fold in the flour. Beat the egg whites until stiff and fold into the egg yolk mixture.

Put the batter into a pastry bag fitted with a ½ inch plain tip. Pipe in 2½ inch long fingers onto greased cookie sheets. Dredge the fingers with sugar.

Bake for 10–12 minutes or until just firm to the touch. Cool on a wire rack.

Ginger Creams

MAKES ABOUT 35

½ cup butter or margarine
⅓ cup firmly packed brown sugar
¼ cup granulated sugar
2 tablespoons molasses
1 tablespoon honey
1 egg
3 cups all-purpose flour
1½ teaspoons ground ginger
FILLING
1¼ cups heavy cream
1 teaspoon grated lemon rind
1 tablespoon sugar

Cream the butter or margarine with the sugars until light and fluffy. Beat in the molasses and honey, followed by the egg. Sift the flour with the ginger and work into the butter mixture to make a smooth dough. Wrap the dough in plastic wrap and chill for 30 minutes.

Preheat the oven to 350°.

Roll out the dough very thinly, about 1/16 inch. Cut into 2½ inch rounds and arrange on greased cookie sheets. Bake for 10–12 minutes or until just firm to the touch. Cool on a wire rack.

To make the filling, whip the cream with the lemon rind and sugar until stiff. Put the cookies together in pairs with the cream filling. Serve soon after assembling or the cookies will soften.

Coffee Whirls

MAKES ABOUT 24

1 cup butter or margarine
½ cup confectioner's sugar, sifted
2 tablespoons strong black coffee
1½ cups all-purpose flour
½ cup cornstarch
FILLING
6 tablespoons butter or margarine
1½ cups confectioner's sugar, sifted
2 tablespoons strong black coffee

Preheat the oven to 375°.

Cream the butter or margarine until softened, then gradually beat in the sugar. Beat in the coffee. Sift the flour with the cornstarch and work into the butter mixture.

Put the dough into a cookie press and form whirls or stars on greased cookie sheets. Bake for 10–15 minutes or until golden brown. Let cool on the cookie sheets for 5 minutes, then remove to a wire rack to cool completely.

To make the filling, cream the butter or margarine until softened, then gradually beat in the sugar alternately with the coffee. Put the cookies together in pairs with the filling.

Rum, Fruit and Nut Cookies

MAKES ABOUT 30

¾ cup butter or margarine
½ cup firmly packed brown sugar
¼ cup granulated sugar
2 eggs
½ teaspoon rum flavoring
¾ cup all-purpose flour, sifted
½ teaspoon ground allspice
¾ cup ground almonds
½ cup chopped toasted filberts
2 tablespoons finely chopped candied
  cherries
⅓ cup chopped mixed candied fruit
  peel
FILLING
4 tablespoons butter or margarine
1 cup confectioner's sugar, sifted
½ teaspoon rum flavoring
1 teaspoon grated orange rind
2 drops yellow food coloring

Preheat the oven to 350°.

Cream the butter or margarine with the sugars until light and fluffy. Beat in the eggs, rum flavoring, flour, allspice and ground almonds. Fold in the nuts, cherries and fruit peel.

Drop teaspoonfuls of the batter onto greased cookie sheets, spacing them well apart. Bake for 10–15 minutes or until the edges are golden brown. Cool on a wire rack.

To make the filling, cream the butter or margarine until soft, then gradually beat in the confectioner's sugar. Beat in the rum flavoring, orange rind and food coloring.

Put the cookies together in pairs with the filling.

Edwardian Cookies

MAKES ABOUT 25

2 cups all-purpose flour
1 teaspoon baking powder
¼ teaspoon salt
½ cup sugar
¾ cup butter or margarine
2 egg yolks
1 teaspoon almond extract
¼ cup apricot or peach jam, warmed
  and strained
walnut halves or blanched almonds
  for decoration
FROSTING
1½ cups confectioner's sugar
4 squares (1 oz each) semisweet
  chocolate, melted with 2 teaspoons
  water
¼ cup heavy cream

Sift the flour, baking powder, salt and sugar into a bowl. Cut in the butter or margarine until the mixture resembles fine bread crumbs. Add the egg yolks and almond extract and mix to a smooth dough. Wrap in plastic wrap and chill for 30 minutes.

Preheat the oven to 375°.

Roll out the dough to ⅛ inch thick. Cut into 1½ inch rounds and arrange on cookie sheets. Bake for 10–12 minutes or until golden brown. Cool on a wire rack.

To make the frosting, sift the confectioner's sugar into a bowl. Beat in the chocolate and cream to make a stiff frosting.

Put cookies together in pairs with the jam. Spread the frosting over the tops and place a walnut half or almond in the center of each.

Filled Orange Cookies

MAKES ABOUT 12

½ cup butter or margarine
½ cup sugar
1 egg yolk
grated rind of 1 orange
2 cups all-purpose flour
FILLING
4 tablespoons butter or margarine
1 cup confectioner's sugar, sifted
1 teaspoon grated orange rind
1 tablespoon orange juice
confectioner's sugar for dredging

Preheat the oven to 375°.

Cream the butter or margarine with the sugar until light and fluffy. Beat in the egg yolk and orange rind, then work in the flour to make a soft dough.

Roll out the dough to ¼ inch thick. Cut into 2 inch rounds and arrange on greased cookie sheets. Bake for 15 minutes or until the edges are lightly browned. Cool on a wire rack.

To make the filling, cream the butter or margarine until soft, then gradually beat in the confectioner's sugar. Beat in the orange rind and juice.

Put the cookies together in pairs with the filling, then dredge with confectioner's sugar.

Edwardian Cookies

Filled Orange Cookies

Chapter Four

COOKIE CLASSICS

Coffee Walnut Cookies

MAKES ABOUT 2 DOZEN

1½ cups ground walnuts
⅓ cup firmly packed brown sugar
¼ cup granulated sugar
1 tablespoon strong black coffee
3 egg whites

Preheat the oven to 375°.

Place the walnuts, sugars and coffee in a bowl and mix well. Beat the egg whites until stiff. Stir about 2 tablespoons of the egg whites into the walnut mixture, then fold in the remainder gently but thoroughly with a metal spoon.

Drop by heaped teaspoonfuls onto cookie sheets lined with edible rice paper, leaving room for spreading. Bake for 15–20 minutes or until golden and crisp.

Let cool on the cookie sheets, then cut the rice paper around each cookie.

Rich Praline Cookies

MAKES ABOUT 1 DOZEN

3 egg whites
½ cup finely chopped toasted almonds
½ cup ground almonds
2 tablespoons all-purpose flour
6 tablespoons sugar
2 tablespoons butter or margarine,
  melted
FILLING
½ cup butter or margarine
2 egg yolks
1 square (1 oz) semisweet chocolate,
  melted
⅓ cup water
5 tablespoons sugar
½ cup blanched almonds

Preheat the oven to 425°.

Beat the egg whites until stiff. Add the nuts, flour, sugar and butter or margarine and fold in gently with a metal spoon.

Drop by heaped teaspoonfuls onto greased cookie sheets, well spaced apart, and flatten into thin rounds with a spatula. Bake for 5 minutes or until golden. Cool on a wire rack.

To make the filling, beat the butter or margarine and egg yolks together until smooth. Beat in the chocolate.

Place the water and sugar in a saucepan and bring to a boil, stirring to dissolve the sugar. Stir in the almonds and boil until the mixture turns light brown. Pour onto a greased cookie sheet or heatproof surface and let cool.

When the praline has cooled and hardened, crush it to a fine powder with a rolling pin. Add to the chocolate mixture and stir well. Refrigerate for 15 minutes.

Put the cookies together in pairs with the filling.

Peppermint Clouds

MAKES ABOUT 3 DOZEN

1 cup sugar
4 eggs
6 drops of peppermint flavoring
1½ cups all-purpose flour, sifted

Preheat the oven to 350°.

Spread out the sugar on a cookie sheet. Place in the oven and bake for 5 minutes. Remove from the oven.

Increase the oven temperature to 400°.

Place the sugar in a bowl and add the eggs. Beat until very pale and thick. Add the peppermint flavoring and flour and mix well.

Drop by tablespoonfuls onto greased cookie sheets, leaving room for spreading. Bake for 15–20 minutes or until light golden brown. Cool on a wire rack.

Langues De Chats

MAKES ABOUT 2 DOZEN

4 tablespoons butter or margarine
¼ cup sugar
2 egg whites
½ cup all-purpose flour, sifted
½ teaspoon vanilla

Preheat the oven to 400°.

Cream the butter or margarine with the sugar until light and fluffy. Beat the egg whites until stiff. Add the egg whites to the creamed mixture alternately with the flour, beating until well combined. Stir in the vanilla.

Fill a cookie press with the dough and form 2½ inch long strips on greased and floured cookie sheets. Bake for 10–12 minutes or until pale golden with the edges just tinged brown.

Let cool on the cookie sheets for 5 minutes, then remove to a wire rack to cool completely.

Frosted Almond Cookies

MAKES ABOUT 2 DOZEN

1 cup all-purpose flour
⅓ cup ground almonds
¼ cup sugar
6 tablespoons butter or margarine
2 egg yolks
¼ teaspoon almond extract
2 tablespoons water
FROSTING
¾ cup confectioner's sugar
1 egg white, beaten until frothy
1 teaspoon all-purpose flour
½ cup sliced almonds

Sift the flour, almonds and sugar into a bowl. Cut in the butter or margarine until the mixture resembles fine crumbs. Add the egg yolks, almond extract and water and mix well. Refrigerate for 30 minutes.

Preheat the oven to 350°.

To make the frosting, mix together all the ingredients to a thick paste.

Roll the chilled dough into walnut-size balls and arrange on greased cookie sheets, well spaced apart. Flatten and hollow the balls slightly with your thumb. Spoon the frosting into the hollows.

Bake for 10–15 minutes or until pale brown around the edges. Cool on a wire rack.

Florentines

MAKES ABOUT 2 DOZEN

½ cup butter or margarine
½ cup sugar
2 tablespoons honey
½ cup sliced almonds
⅓ cup chopped candied cherries
⅓ cup chopped candied fruit peel
1 cup all-purpose flour, sifted
4 squares (1 oz each) semisweet
  chocolate, melted

Preheat the oven to 350°.

Place the butter or margarine, sugar and honey in a saucepan and heat, stirring, until melted and smooth. Remove from the heat and stir in the almonds, candied cherries, fruit peel and flour. Mix well.

Drop by heaped teaspoonfuls onto cookie sheets lined with parchment paper, leaving room for spreading. Bake for 10 minutes. Let cool on the cookie sheets.

Carefully remove the cookies from the cookie sheets. Spread the chocolate over the undersides and mark in a wavy pattern with a fork. Let set on a wire rack.

Florentines

Butter Coconut Cookies

MAKES ABOUT 4 DOZEN

1 cup butter or margarine
¾ cup sugar
1 egg
2 tablespoons rum
3 cups all-purpose flour
½ teaspoon salt
¼ cup shredded coconut

Cream the butter or margarine with the sugar until light and fluffy. Beat in the egg and rum. Sift the flour and salt into the bowl and mix well.

Form the dough into a roll about 2½ inches in diameter. Wrap in wax paper and refrigerate for 4 hours.

Preheat the oven to 350°.

Cut the roll of dough into ⅛ inch thick slices and arrange on ungreased cookie sheets. Bake for 10 minutes or until golden brown.

Remove the cookies to a wire rack and sprinkle over the coconut. Let cool.

Crunchy Topped Almond Cookies

MAKES ABOUT 2 DOZEN

½ cup butter or margarine
2 cups sugar
4 eggs
¼ cup kirsch
4 cups all-purpose flour
½ teaspoon salt
1 cup ground almonds
½ cup finely chopped almonds

Cream the butter or margarine with 1¾ cups of the sugar until light and fluffy. Beat in three of the eggs and the kirsch. Sift the flour, salt and ground almonds into the bowl and mix well. Refrigerate for 30 minutes.

Preheat the oven to 375°.

Roll out the dough on a floured surface to ¼ inch thick. Cut out 3 inch rounds and arrange on greased cookie sheets.

Mix the remaining sugar with the chopped almonds. Lightly beat the remaining egg. Brush the egg over the cookies and sprinkle the almond mixture on top.

Bake for 15–20 minutes or until golden brown. Let cool on the cookie sheets for 5 minutes, then remove to a wire rack to cool completely.

Honey Filbert Cookies

MAKES ABOUT 2 DOZEN

½ cup butter or margarine
5 tablespoons sugar
¾ cup ground filberts
1¼ cups all-purpose flour
¼ cup honey
4 squares (1 oz each) semisweet or
  milk chocolate, melted

Preheat the oven to 350°.

Cream the butter or margarine with the sugar until light and fluffy. Beat in the nuts. Sift the flour into the bowl and mix to a soft dough. If the dough is too dry, add a little water. Refrigerate for 30 minutes.

Roll out the dough on a floured surface to ¼ inch thick. Cut out decorative shapes with floured cookie cutters and arrange on greased cookie sheets. Bake for 12–15 minutes or until golden brown. Cool on a wire rack.

Put the cookies together in pairs with the honey. Spread the chocolate over the tops of the cookies and let set.

Fig and Filbert Crisps

MAKES ABOUT 3½ DOZEN

2 cups all-purpose flour
⅛ teaspoon salt
1 teaspoon baking powder
¼ teaspoon grated nutmeg
6 tablespoons butter or margarine
⅔ cup firmly packed brown sugar
1 egg, lightly beaten
3 tablespoons heavy cream
8 dried figs, finely chopped
½ cup chopped toasted filberts

Preheat the oven to 350°.

Sift the flour, salt, baking powder and nutmeg into a bowl. Cut in the butter or margarine until the mixture resembles fine crumbs. Stir in the sugar.

Add the egg and cream and mix well. Stir in the figs and nuts.

Roll out the dough on a floured surface to ⅛ inch thick. Cut into 1½ inch rounds and arrange on greased cookie sheets, leaving room for spreading.

Bake for 10–15 minutes or until golden brown. Cool on a wire rack.

Almond Petits Fours

MAKES ABOUT 2½ DOZEN

2 egg whites
6 tablespoons sugar
1 cup ground almonds
2 drops of almond extract
halved candied cherries
chopped candied angelica

Preheat the oven to 350°.

Beat the egg whites until stiff. Add the sugar, ground almonds and almond extract and fold together gently but thoroughly with a metal spoon.

Put the mixture into a pastry bag fitted with a star tip. Pipe half the mixture onto greased cookie sheets in stars and the rest into "S" shapes. Top the stars with candied cherry halves and the "S" shapes with chopped angelica.

Bake for about 20 minutes or until light golden brown. Cool on a wire rack.

Filbert Macaroons

MAKES ABOUT 1½ DOZEN

3 egg whites
1 cup sugar
1½ cups ground filberts
1 teaspoon vanilla
1 teaspoon grated lemon rind

Beat the egg whites until frothy. Gradually beat in the sugar and continue beating until the mixture is stiff and glossy. Gently fold in the filberts, vanilla and lemon rind with a metal spoon.

Drop by heaped teaspoonfuls onto cookie sheets lined with parchment paper, leaving room for spreading. Set aside for 1½ hours.

Preheat the oven to 350°.

Bake for 15 minutes or until firm to the touch. Let cool on the cookie sheets.

**Almond Petits Fours and
Rum Truffles (page 148)**

Filbert Macaroons

Chocolate Coconut Macaroons

MAKES ABOUT 4 DOZEN

2 squares (1 oz each) semisweet
  chocolate
½ cup sugar
½ cup shredded coconut
¼ teaspoon vanilla
2 tablespoons heavy cream
2 egg whites
⅛ teaspoon salt

Preheat the oven to 350°.

Melt the chocolate over low heat in a heavy-based saucepan. Remove from the heat and stir in the sugar, coconut, vanilla and cream. Let cool completely.

Beat the egg whites with the salt until stiff. Add the chocolate mixture and fold together gently but thoroughly with a metal spoon.

Drop by heaped teaspoonfuls onto cookie sheets lined with parchment, leaving room for spreading. Bake for 15–20 minutes or until firm to the touch. Let cool on the cookie sheets.

Marzipan Cookies

MAKES ABOUT 1½ DOZEN

½ cup sugar
¾ cup ground almonds
grated rind of 1 small orange
2 egg yolks
⅛ teaspoon almond extract
¼ cup confectioner's sugar
¼ cup sliced almonds

Preheat the oven to 375°.

Place the sugar, ground almonds and orange rind in a bowl and stir together. Add the egg yolks and almond extract and mix with your fingertips to a smooth paste. Refrigerate for 10 minutes.

Sprinkle the confectioner's sugar over a work surface. Roll out the almond paste on the sugared surface with a sugared rolling pin to about ⅛ inch thick. Cut out 2 inch rounds and arrange on greased cookie sheets. Press a few sliced almonds into each cookie.

Bake for 8–10 minutes or until golden. Cool on a wire rack.

Coffee Liqueur Cookies

MAKES ABOUT 2 DOZEN

2 cups all-purpose flour
¼ teaspoon salt
½ cup butter or margarine
⅓ cup firmly packed brown sugar
2 egg yolks
¼ cup coffee liqueur

Sift the flour and salt into a bowl. Cut in the butter or margarine until the mixture resembles fine crumbs. Stir in the sugar. Add the egg yolks and liqueur and mix to a soft dough. Refrigerate for 30 minutes.

Preheat the oven to 400°.

Roll out the dough on a floured surface to ¼ inch thick. Cut out 2 inch rounds and arrange on greased cookie sheets.

Bake for 12–15 minutes or until golden brown around the edges. Let cool on the cookie sheets for 5 minutes, then remove to a wire rack to cool completely.

Chocolate Rum Cookies

MAKES ABOUT 5 DOZEN

1 cup butter or margarine
2 cups firmly packed brown sugar
1 egg
1 egg yolk
½ teaspoon vanilla
¾ cup milk
3 tablespoons rum
3½ cups all-purpose flour
2 teaspoons baking soda
½ teaspoon salt
4 squares (1 oz each) semisweet
  chocolate, melted
1 cup chopped almonds

Preheat the oven to 350°.

Cream the butter or margarine with the sugar until light and fluffy. Beat in the egg, egg yolk, vanilla, milk and rum. Sift the flour, soda and salt into the bowl. Add the chocolate and mix well. Stir in the almonds.

Drop by heaped teaspoonfuls onto greased cookie sheets, leaving room for spreading. Bake for 10–15 minutes or until just firm to the touch. Let cool on the cookie sheets for 5 minutes, then remove to a wire rack to cool completely.

Almond Tuiles

MAKES ABOUT 4 DOZEN

2 large egg whites
½ **cup sugar**
½ **cup all-purpose flour**
¼ **cup ground almonds**
4 tablespoons butter or margarine,
  melted
½ **teaspoon vanilla**

Preheat the oven to 350°.

Beat the egg whites until frothy. Gradually beat in the sugar and continue beating until the mixture is stiff and glossy. Sift in the flour and almonds. Add the butter or margarine and vanilla. Beat until well combined.

Drop by heaped teaspoonfuls onto greased cookie sheets, leaving room for spreading. Bake for 6–7 minutes or until golden brown. Lift the cookies off the cookie sheets with a spatula and lay over a rolling pin, bottle or other rounded shape so that they are curved. Let cool.

Variation
Russian Cigarette Cookies: Omit the ground almonds. Bake as above, allowing 7–8 minutes, but bake only two cookies at a time. Let cool on the cookie sheet for a few seconds, then quickly wind around a pencil. Slide off onto a wire rack to cool.

Almond Tuiles Step by Step

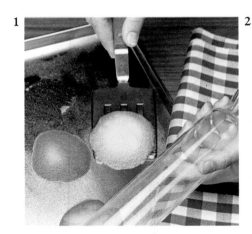

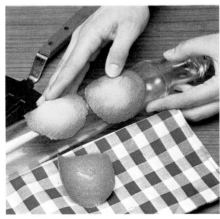

1. To shape the tuiles, cool slightly. Have a rolling pin, bottle or other rounded shape handy.
2. Lay the tuiles over the rounded shape to make the traditional curved shape of a roof tile.

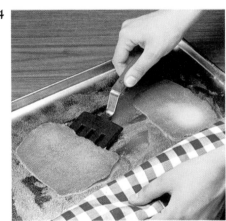

3. For Russian Cigarette Cookies, bake the cookie dough until golden brown.
4. Let cool on the cookie sheet for a few seconds, then lift off with a spatula.

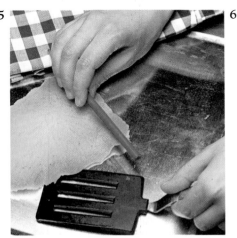

5. Invert the cookie onto a flat surface and place a pencil or similar object on one short side.
6. Roll the cookie around the pencil to make a cigarette shape. Slide off onto a wire rack to cool.

Ratafia Cookies

MAKES 4–5 DOZEN

4 tablespoons butter or margarine
1½ cups sugar
1 teaspoon apricot brandy
2 cups ground almonds
2 egg whites

Preheat the oven to 350°.

Cream the butter or margarine with the sugar until light and fluffy. Stir in the apricot brandy and ground almonds. Beat the egg whites until stiff and fold into the almond mixture with a metal spoon.

Put the mixture into a pastry bag fitted with a 1 inch star tip. Pipe in stars onto cookie sheets lined with edible rice paper, leaving room for spreading.

Bake for 25–30 minutes or until golden brown and firm to the touch. Let cool on the cookie sheets for 5 minutes, then cut the rice paper around each cookie. Remove to a wire rack to cool completely.

Orange Chocolate Cookies

MAKES ABOUT 1½ DOZEN

¾ cup ground almonds
1 cup all-purpose flour, sifted
¼ cup sugar
¼ cup unsweetened cocoa
⅛ teaspoon salt
grated rind of 2 oranges
1 egg yolk
1 teaspoon orange juice
½ cup butter or margarine, melted
¼ cup milk
10 blanched almonds, halved

Preheat the oven to 375°.

Mix together the ground almonds, flour, sugar, cocoa, salt and orange rind.

Lightly beat the egg yolk with the orange juice and butter or margarine. Add to the ground almond mixture with the milk and mix to a soft dough.

Drop by heaped teaspoonfuls onto greased cookie sheets, well spaced apart. Flatten with a fork and press an almond half into each cookie.

Bake for 30–35 minutes or until firm to the touch. Cool on a wire rack.

Orangines

MAKES ABOUT 3½ DOZEN

4 tablespoons butter or margarine
¼ cup sugar
⅓ cup all-purpose flour
⅓ cup chopped candied orange peel
½ cup sliced almonds
2 tablespoons milk

Preheat the oven to 375°.

Cream the butter or margarine with the sugar until light and fluffy. Sift the flour into the bowl and mix well. Mix in the orange peel, almonds and milk.

Drop by teaspoonfuls onto greased cookie sheets, well spaced apart. Flatten with a fork dipped in cold water.

Bake for 10 minutes or until lightly browned. Let cool on the cookie sheets for 5 minutes, then remove to a wire rack to cool completely.

Wine Currant Cookies

MAKES 2½–3 DOZEN

⅔ cup currants
½ cup sweet white wine
¾ cup butter or margarine
¾ cup sugar
2 eggs, lightly beaten
3 cups all-purpose flour
1½ teaspoons ground cinnamon

Place the currants in a bowl. Pour the wine over and let soak for 1 hour.

Preheat the oven to 375°.

Cream the butter or margarine with the sugar until light and fluffy. Beat in the eggs. Sift the flour and cinnamon into the bowl. Add the currants and wine and mix well.

Drop by heaped teaspoonfuls onto greased cookie sheets, leaving room for spreading. Bake for 15–20 minutes or until golden brown.

Let cool on the cookie sheets for 5 minutes, then remove to a wire rack to cool completely.

Madeleines

MAKES 36

4 eggs
½ cup sugar
½ teaspoon vanilla
1 cup all-purpose flour, sifted
½ cup butter or margarine, melted

Preheat the oven to 400°.

Beat the eggs, sugar and vanilla until very thick and pale. Fold in the flour and melted butter or margarine.

Divide the batter among 36 greased and floured madeleine molds (shell-shaped molds). The molds should be only three-quarters full. Bake for 7–10 minutes or until a wooden toothpick inserted into the center comes out clean.

Let cool in the molds for 5 minutes, then invert onto a wire rack to cool completely.

Brandy Lace Roll-Ups

MAKES ABOUT 12

4 tablespoons butter or margarine
3 tablespoons light corn syrup
¼ cup sugar
1 teaspoon brandy
½ cup all-purpose flour, sifted
½ teaspoon ground ginger
grated rind of ½ lemon

Preheat the oven to 350°.

Place the butter or margarine, syrup and sugar in a saucepan and heat until melted and smooth. Remove from the heat and stir in the remaining ingredients.

Drop by teaspoonfuls onto greased cookie sheets, leaving room for spreading. Bake for 8 minutes.

Remove the cookies from the cookie sheets one at a time and roll around an oiled wooden spoon handle. Slide off onto a wire rack and let cool.

If the cookies become too hard to roll, return them to the oven for 1–2 minutes.

Brandy Lace Roll-Ups

Chapter Five

AROUND THE WORLD COOKIES

German Spice Squares

MAKES ABOUT 3 DOZEN

3 large eggs
1 cup firmly packed brown sugar
½ cup honey
3 cups all-purpose flour
½ teaspoon salt
1 teaspoon baking powder
½ teaspoon ground ginger
½ teaspoon ground cinnamon
¼ teaspoon grated nutmeg
¼ teaspoon ground cloves
2 tablespoons unsweetened cocoa

Preheat the oven to 350°.

Place the eggs, sugar and honey in a bowl and beat until well combined. Sift the flour, salt, baking powder, spices and cocoa into the bowl and mix to a smooth batter.

Pour into a greased 9 inch square cake pan. Smooth the surface. Bake for 30 minutes or until a wooden pick inserted into the center comes out clean.

Cool in the pan, then cut into small 1½ or 2 inch squares to serve.

German Chocolate Pretzels

MAKES 2½ DOZEN

½ cup butter or margarine
¼ cup sugar
1 egg
2 cups all-purpose flour
2 tablespoons unsweetened cocoa
GLAZE
1 tablespoon milk
2 tablespoons sugar
2 squares (1 oz each) semisweet
  chocolate
1 tablespoon light corn syrup
1 teaspoon butter or margarine

Cream the butter or margarine with the sugar until light and fluffy. Beat in the egg. Sift the flour and cocoa into the bowl and mix to a smooth dough. Refrigerate for 30 minutes.

Preheat the oven to 350°.

Divide the dough into 30 pieces and roll into sausages about 12 inches long. Twist into pretzel shapes and arrange on ungreased cookie sheets, leaving room for spreading.

Bake for 10 minutes or until firm to the touch. Cool on a wire rack.

To make the glaze, put the milk, sugar, chocolate and syrup in a saucepan and heat until melted and smooth. Remove the pan from the heat and stir in the butter or margarine. Let cool until just warm. Dip the cookies into the glaze and let set on a wire rack.

German Spice Cookies

MAKES ABOUT 3 DOZEN

½ cup firmly packed brown sugar
2 teaspoons grated lemon rind
1 tablespoon chopped candied citron
  peel
4 tablespoons butter or margarine
1 egg
1¼ cups all-purpose flour
½ teaspoon baking powder
¼ teaspoon black pepper
pinch of salt
1 teaspoon ground cinnamon
½ teaspoon ground allspice
½ teaspoon grated nutmeg

Beat the sugar, lemon rind, candied citron peel and butter or margarine in a bowl until light and fluffy. Beat in the egg. Sift the flour, baking powder, pepper, salt and spices into the bowl and mix well to a firm dough.

Form the dough into two rolls about 1 inch in diameter. Wrap in wax paper and refrigerate overnight.

Preheat the oven to 400°.

Cut the rolls of dough into ½ inch thick slices and arrange on greased cookie sheets, leaving room for spreading. Bake for 10–12 minutes or until light golden and crisp.

Let cool on the cookie sheets for 5 minutes, then remove to a wire rack to cool completely. Store for several days before serving.

German Almond Crescents

MAKES ABOUT 2 DOZEN

1 cup butter or margarine
1 cup + 2 tablespoons sugar
3 eggs
¼ cup sour cream
2½ cups all-purpose flour
1 teaspoon ground cinnamon
1½ teaspoons grated lemon rind
⅓ cup chopped almonds

Cream the butter or margarine with the 1 cup of sugar until light and fluffy. Beat in two of the eggs and the sour cream. Sift the flour and cinnamon into the bowl. Add the lemon rind and mix to a soft dough. Refrigerate for 1 hour.

Preheat the oven to 375°.

Lightly beat the remaining egg. Mix the chopped almonds with the remaining sugar.

Break off small pieces of cookie dough and roll into small sausages with tapered ends. Bend into crescents. Brush with the beaten egg and coat with the almond mixture.

Arrange the crescents on greased cookie sheets, leaving room for spreading. Bake for 10–15 minutes or until firm to the touch. Cool on a wire rack.

Polish Chocolate Matzo Squares

MAKES 8–10

8 squares (1 oz each) semisweet
  chocolate, grated
¼ cup dry dark rye bread crumbs
1 cup sugar
2 eggs
1 cup ground almonds
1¼ cups slivered almonds
⅓ cup finely chopped candied orange
  peel
6 egg whites
2–3 large matzos
FROSTING
⅔ cup heavy cream
1 tablespoon sugar
2 tablespoons unsweetened cocoa
1 tablespoon light corn syrup
4 tablespoons butter

Preheat the oven to 400°.

Mix together the chocolate, bread crumbs, sugar, whole eggs, ground and slivered almonds and orange peel. Beat the egg whites until stiff and fold into the chocolate mixture.

Arrange the matzos over the bottom of a greased 11×7 inch baking pan, cutting them to fit. Pour the batter over and spread it out evenly. Bake for 30 minutes. Cool in the pan.

To make the frosting, put the cream, sugar and cocoa in a heavy-based saucepan and bring to a boil, stirring vigorously. Stir in the syrup. Remove from the heat and stir in the butter until melted. Cool slightly until the frosting has thickened.

Spread the frosting over the chocolate cake. Let set, then cut into squares and remove from the pan. Decorate with almonds and orange peel, if desired.

Polish Chocolate Matzo Squares

British Digestive Biscuits

MAKES ABOUT 2½ DOZEN

1 cup all-purpose flour
2 cups whole wheat or graham flour
½ teaspoon salt
6 tablespoons butter or margarine
6 tablespoons lard or shortening
¼ cup sugar
1 egg
½ cup water

Preheat the oven to 400°.

Sift the flours and salt into a bowl. Cut in the butter or margarine and lard or shortening until the mixture resembles fine crumbs. Stir in the sugar. Add the egg and water and mix to a smooth dough.

Roll out the dough on a floured surface to ¼ inch thick. Cut out 2 inch rounds and arrange on greased cookie sheets.

Bake for 15 minutes or until golden brown. Let cool on the cookie sheets for 5 minutes, then remove to a wire rack to cool.

British Garibaldi Cookies

MAKES ABOUT 1½ DOZEN

2 cups self-rising flour
⅛ teaspoon salt
½ cup butter or margarine
⅓ cup firmly packed brown sugar
¼ cup milk
⅓ cup raisins
⅓ cup currants
1 tablespoon granulated sugar

Sift the flour and salt into a bowl. Cut in the butter or margarine until the mixture resembles fine crumbs. Stir in the brown sugar. Add the milk and mix to a smooth dough. Refrigerate for 30 minutes.

Preheat the oven to 375°.

Divide the dough in half. Roll out one portion on a floured surface to a rectangle about ⅛ inch thick. Square off the sides, then place the dough rectangle on a greased cookie sheet. Sprinkle the raisins and currants over.

Roll out the second portion of dough to a thin rectangle the same size as the first. Place on top of the fruit. Press down lightly with a rolling pin so the fruit nearly shows through the top layer of dough. Score into squares with a sharp knife. Sprinkle the granulated sugar on top.

Bake for 20 minutes or until golden. Let cool on the cookie sheet, then break into squares.

English Jumbles

MAKES ABOUT 2 DOZEN

½ cup butter or margarine
½ cup sugar
1 egg
1 cup all-purpose flour
½ cup ground almonds
grated rind of 1 lemon

Preheat the oven to 400°.

Cream the butter or margarine with the sugar until light and fluffy. Beat in the egg. Sift the flour and almonds into the bowl. Add the lemon rind and mix well.

Pull off small pieces of the dough and roll out to 1½ × ½ inch rectangles. Bend into "S" shapes and arrange on greased cookie sheets, leaving room for spreading.

Bake for 15 minutes or until lightly browned. Let cool on the cookie sheets.

English Almond Cookies

MAKES ABOUT 1 DOZEN

2 tablespoons blanched almonds
1 teaspoon salt
6 tablespoons butter or margarine
6 tablespoons sugar
1 egg yolk
¼ cup milk
1½ cups all-purpose flour
3 tablespoons finely chopped candied cherries

Preheat the broiler.

Spread out the almonds in the broiler pan and sprinkle over the salt. Broil the nuts until they are browned on both sides, shaking the pan to turn the nuts over. Tip the nuts onto a wooden board and chop finely.

Cream the butter or margarine with the sugar until light and fluffy. Beat in the egg yolk and milk. Sift the flour into the bowl. Add the chopped almonds and cherries and mix to a dough. Refrigerate for 30 minutes.

Preheat the oven to 375°.

Roll out the dough on a floured surface to ¼ inch thick. Cut into decorative shapes with floured cookie cutters and arrange on greased cookie sheets.

Bake for 20 minutes or until golden brown. Let cool on the cookie sheets for 5 minutes, then remove to a wire rack to cool completely.

British Melting Moments

MAKES ABOUT 1½ DOZEN

½ cup butter or margarine
½ cup shortening
¾ cup sugar
1 egg
2½ cups all-purpose flour
1 teaspoon baking powder
¼ cup rolled oats

Cream the butter or margarine and shortening with the sugar until light and fluffy. Beat in the egg. Sift the flour and baking powder into the bowl and mix to a smooth dough.

Roll the dough into walnut-size balls and coat with the oats. Arrange on ungreased cookie sheets, well spaced apart, and flatten slightly with a fork. Refrigerate for 30 minutes.

Preheat the oven to 350°.

Bake for 20–25 minutes or until the cookies are golden brown. Let cool on the cookie sheets for 5 minutes, then remove to a wire rack to cool completely.

Danish Cream Cones

MAKES ABOUT 3 DOZEN

6 tablespoons butter or margarine, melted
¼ cup sugar
½ cup all-purpose flour, sifted
1 teaspoon ground ginger
4 egg whites
FILLING
1 cup heavy cream
2 tablespoons confectioner's sugar
1 tablespoon Madeira
2 tablespoons chopped preserved stem ginger

Preheat the oven to 400°.

Place the butter or margarine, sugar, flour and ginger in a bowl and beat until smooth. Beat the egg whites until stiff. Add to the ginger mixture and fold together gently but thoroughly with a metal spoon.

Drop by teaspoonfuls onto greased cookie sheets, leaving plenty of space for spreading. Flatten gently with a spoon.

Bake for 3–5 minutes or until light golden. Remove one at a time with a spatula and shape into cones with your fingers. Cool on a wire rack.

If the cookies become too firm to shape into cones, return them to the oven for 1–2 minutes to soften.

To make the filling, whip the cream with the sugar until thick. Fold in the Madeira and ginger. Fill the cold cone cookies with the cream mixture just before serving.

British Melting Moments

Danish Cream Cones

Scandinavian Red Currant Cream Cookies

MAKES ABOUT 10

2 cups all-purpose flour
½ teaspoon salt
¼ cup sugar
2 egg yolks
¾ cup butter or margarine, softened
FILLING
1 egg, separated
2 tablespoons sugar
1½ teaspoons cornstarch
2 teaspoons all-purpose flour
¾ cup milk
¼ teaspoon vanilla
TOPPING
1½ cups confectioner's sugar
¼ teaspoon lemon flavoring
2–3 tablespoons warm water
⅓ cup red currant jelly

Sift the flour, salt and sugar into a bowl. Make a well in the center and put in the egg yolks and butter or margarine. Use your fingertips to work the egg yolks and fat together, then gradually work in the flour to make a smooth dough. Wrap the dough in plastic wrap and chill for 1 hour.

Meanwhile, make the filling. Beat the egg yolk with the sugar until creamy. Gradually beat in the cornstarch and flour, then stir in about one-quarter of the milk and the vanilla.

Scald the remaining milk and gradually beat it into the egg yolk mixture. Pour into the saucepan and bring to a boil, stirring constantly. Remove from the heat and beat the mixture until smooth. Let cool slightly.

Beat the egg white until stiff and fold into the warm custard mixture. Cook over low heat for 2 minutes, stirring occasionally. Let cool completely.

Preheat the oven to 375°.

Roll out the dough thinly. Cut into 3 inch rounds and arrange on greased cookie sheets. Bake for 7 minutes or until golden brown. Cool on a wire rack.

Put the cookies together in pairs with the filling.

To make the topping, sift the confectioner's sugar into a bowl. Add the lemon flavoring and water and stir to make a thick frosting. Spread the frosting over the tops of the cookies and place a blob of red currant jelly in the center. Let set.

Scandinavian Port Cookies

MAKES ABOUT 3 DOZEN

3 cups all-purpose flour
2 teaspoons baking powder
¼ teaspoon salt
¼ teaspoon ground mace
½ teaspoon ground ginger
¼ teaspoon ground cloves
1 cup sugar
¾ cup ground almonds
4 tablespoons butter or margarine
2 eggs
6 tablespoons milk
¼ cup port wine
½ cup sliced almonds

Preheat the oven to 350°.

Sift the flour, baking powder, salt, spices, sugar and ground almonds into a bowl. Cut in the butter or margarine until the mixture resembles fine crumbs. Add the eggs, milk and port and mix to a smooth dough.

Roll out the dough on a floured surface to ¼ inch thick. Cut out 2½ inch rounds and arrange on greased cookie sheets. Press a few almond slices into each cookie.

Bake for 15–20 minutes or until golden brown around the edges. Cool on a wire rack.

Scandinavian Cardamom Cookies

MAKES ABOUT 4 DOZEN

¾ cup butter or margarine
1⅓ cups firmly packed brown sugar
1 egg
¼ cup light cream
½ teaspoon almond extract
4 cups all-purpose flour
1 teaspoon baking powder
2 teaspoons ground cardamom

Cream the butter or margarine with the sugar until light and fluffy. Beat in the egg, cream and almond extract. Sift the flour, baking powder and cardamom into the bowl and mix to a smooth dough.

Form the dough into a roll about 2 inches in diameter. Wrap in wax paper and refrigerate overnight.

Preheat the oven to 400°.

Cut the roll of dough into ¼ inch thick slices and arrange on greased cookie sheets. Bake for about 12 minutes or until just tinged brown. Cool on a wire rack.

Scandinavian Butter Cookies

MAKES ABOUT 5 DOZEN

1 cup butter or margarine
½ cup sugar
2 egg yolks
½ teaspoon almond extract
¼ teaspoon vanilla
2½ cups all-purpose flour
½ teaspoon salt

Preheat the oven to 375°.

Cream the butter or margarine with the sugar until light and fluffy. Beat in the egg yolks, almond extract and vanilla. Sift the flour and salt into the bowl and mix well.

Fill a cookie press with the dough. Using a small star plate, make "S" shapes about 1½ inches long on ungreased cookie sheets.

Bake for 10–15 minutes or until just firm to the touch and golden brown around the edges. Let cool on the cookie sheets for 5 minutes, then remove to a wire rack to cool completely.

Dutch Mirror Cookies

MAKES ABOUT 2 DOZEN

1¾ cups all-purpose flour
1 teaspoon baking powder
½ teaspoon salt
½ teaspoon ground cloves
½ teaspoon ground ginger
½ teaspoon ground cinnamon
½ teaspoon ground cardamom
½ teaspoon ground coriander
¾ cup butter or margarine
⅔ cup firmly packed brown sugar
1 tablespoon milk
1 cup chopped almonds

Sift the flour, baking powder, salt and spices into a bowl. Cut in the butter or margarine until the mixture resembles fine crumbs. Add the sugar and milk and mix to a smooth dough. Work in the almonds. Let rest overnight.

Preheat the oven to 350°.

Roll out the dough on a floured surface to ⅛ inch thick. Using a speculaas mold (see below) or other cookie cutters, cut out figures or fancy shapes. Arrange on greased cookie sheets.

Bake for 15–20 minutes or until crisp and brown. Cool on a wire rack.

Note: A speculaas mold shows two figures or shapes that mirror each other. The traditional mold is a pair of lovers kissing.

Scandinavian Butter Cookies

French Pastry Butterflies

MAKES ABOUT 5 DOZEN

2 cups all-purpose flour
¼ teaspoon salt
1 cup sweet butter, well chilled
½ cup ice water
½ cup sugar

Sift the flour and salt into a bowl. Cut in 4 tablespoons of the butter until the mixture resembles fine crumbs. Add enough of the water to make a firm dough. Refrigerate for 15 minutes.

Place the remaining butter between two pieces of wax paper and pound with a rolling pin to a slab about ¾ inch thick.

Roll out the dough on a floured surface to an oblong about ¼ inch thick. Place the slab of butter in the center and fold the dough over it to make a package. Refrigerate for 10 minutes.

Place the dough package, seam down, on the floured surface and roll out into an oblong again. Fold into three, then turn so the folds are to the side. Roll out into an oblong again. Fold into three. Refrigerate for 15 minutes. Repeat the rolling out and folding process twice.

Roll out the dough to a 15×4 inch rectangle, ⅛ inch thick. Sprinkle half the sugar over. Fold the long sides in to meet in the center and press down gently. Sprinkle half the remaining sugar over. Fold the long sides over again to meet in the center. Sprinkle the remaining sugar over, then fold the two long sides up to meet and press them together firmly. You should now have a 1 inch wide strip, about 15 inches long.

Cut the strip into ¼ inch thick slices. Arrange, cut sides down, on greased cookie sheets, well spaced apart. Gently pull each slice open to make a "V" shape and flatten slightly with the heel of your hand. Refrigerate for 10 minutes.

Preheat the oven to 400°.

Bake for 7 minutes, then turn the cookies over and bake for 7 minutes longer or until they are deep golden brown and the sugar has caramelized. Cool on a wire rack.

French Pastry Twists

MAKES ABOUT 1 DOZEN

1 cup all-purpose flour
⅛ teaspoon salt
½ cup sweet butter, well chilled
¼ cup ice water
½ cup chopped almonds
2 tablespoons confectioner's sugar

Make the pastry dough following the instructions given in the recipe for French Pastry Butterflies (page 100). Refrigerate for 15 minutes.

Preheat the oven to 425°.

Roll out the dough on a floured surface to a 6×8 inch rectangle. Sprinkle the almonds over the dough, then dredge with the confectioner's sugar. Gently press the almonds and sugar into the dough with a rolling pin.

Cut the dough into ¾ inch wide strips. Holding each strip by the ends with the thumb and forefinger, make two twists, almost to enclose the nut topping. Arrange the twists on a dampened cookie sheet, leaving room for spreading.

Bake for 10–15 minutes or until golden brown. Cool on a wire rack.

French Chocolate Meringue Leaves

MAKES ABOUT 2 DOZEN

3 egg whites
6 tablespoons sugar
¾ cup ground almonds
¼ teaspoon almond extract
3 squares (1 oz each) semisweet
  chocolate, melted

Preheat the oven to 350°.

Beat the egg whites until frothy. Gradually beat in the sugar and continue beating until the mixture is stiff and glossy. Fold in the almonds and almond extract with a metal spoon.

Drop by teaspoonfuls onto cookie sheets lined with parchment paper, leaving space for spreading. Bake for 10–15 minutes or until set and golden brown.

Lift off the cookie sheets, on the paper, and place cookie side down on a wire rack. Let cool, then carefully peel off the paper.

Spread the chocolate over the smooth side of each cookie. Mark leaf veins with a toothpick and let set.

Scotch Shortbread

MAKES 6–8

1 cup all-purpose flour
½ cup rice flour
pinch of salt
¼ cup + 1 tablespoon sugar
½ cup butter or margarine

Sift the flour, rice flour and salt into a bowl. Stir in the ¼ cup of sugar. Cut in the butter or margarine until the mixture resembles fine crumbs. Mix to a smooth dough. Refrigerate for 10 minutes.

Preheat the oven to 325°.

Press the dough into a floured shortbread mold with the heel of your hand. Alternatively, press over the bottom of a floured 8 inch layer cake pan. Invert onto a greased cookie sheet. If you have used a cake pan to shape the dough into a round, flute the edges. Score into six to eight wedges.

Bake for 45 minutes or until pale golden and firm to the touch. Let cool on the cookie sheet for 10 minutes, then remove to a wire rack to cool completely.

Sprinkle the remaining sugar over and break into the wedges to serve.

Note: If desired, the shortbread dough may be rolled out to ¼ inch thick and cut into rounds or other shapes with floured cookie cutters. Reduce the baking time to about 20 minutes.

Scotch Shortbread Step by Step

1. Press the shortbread dough into a floured shortbread mold with the heel of your hand. The traditional wooden molds usually have a raised motif of a thistle or game bird on the bottom.
2. Hold the wooden mold close to a greased cookie sheet and tap the base; the molded shortbread dough should come out easily.

3. If you shape the dough in a floured layer cake pan, flute the edge so that it looks frilly. You can also decorate the top with rings of small holes. Use a skewer, and a glass and saucer as guides.
4. Score the shortbread round into six or eight portions using a sharp knife. These triangular wedges with their frilly edge are traditionally known as "petticoat tails".

5. Bake the shortbread until it is pale golden and firm to the touch.
6. Let cool on the cookie sheet for 10 minutes, then remove to a wire rack to cool completely.

Italian Cornmeal Cookies

MAKES ABOUT 4 DOZEN

⅔ cup golden raisins
¼ cup rum
1¼ cups all-purpose flour
2 cups yellow cornmeal
½ teaspoon salt
⅓ cup butter or margarine
½ cup sugar
2 eggs
¼ teaspoon vanilla
grated rind of 1 lemon
confectioner's sugar

Preheat the oven to 375°.

Place the raisins in a bowl and sprinkle the rum over. Let soak.

Sift the flour, cornmeal and salt into a bowl. Cut in the butter or margarine until the mixture resembles fine crumbs. Stir in the sugar. Add the eggs, vanilla and lemon rind and mix well. Mix in the rum and raisins.

Break off small pieces of the dough and shape into 2 × 1 inch oblongs. Slightly flatten each one with your thumb and arrange on greased cookie sheets.

Bake for 15 minutes or until golden. Cool on a wire rack. Sprinkle with confectioner's sugar before serving.

Spanish Sesame and Anise Seed Cookies

MAKES ABOUT 2 DOZEN

1½ cups vegetable oil
thinly pared rind of ½ lemon
1 tablespoon sesame seeds
1 tablespoon anise seed
½ cup dry white wine
2 teaspoons grated lemon rind
2 teaspoons grated orange rind
½ cup sugar
5 cups all-purpose flour
1 teaspoon ground cinnamon
1 teaspoon ground cloves
1 teaspoon ground ginger
¼ cup sliced almonds

Heat the oil in a saucepan. Stir in the pared lemon rind, sesame seeds and anise seed and remove from the heat. Let cool, then discard the lemon rind.

Pour the oil mixture into a bowl and add the wine, lemon and orange rinds and sugar. Stir to mix. Sift the flour and spices into the bowl and mix to a smooth dough. Let rest for 30 minutes.

Preheat the oven to 400°.

Roll the dough into walnut-size balls. Arrange on greased and floured cookie sheets, well spaced apart, and flatten with the heel of your hand to about ½ inch thick. Press a few almond slices into the top of each cookie.

Bake for 15–20 minutes or until firm to the touch and golden brown around the edges.

Cool on a wire rack.

Spanish Sherry Cookies

MAKES ABOUT 3 DOZEN

2 cups all-purpose flour
½ teaspoon salt
½ cup sugar
1 teaspoon anise seed
grated rind of 1 lemon
1 egg
2 tablespoons vegetable oil
¼ cup sweet sherry

Preheat the oven to 425°.

Sift the flour, salt and sugar into a bowl. Stir in the anise seed and lemon rind. Add the egg, oil and sherry and mix to a smooth dough.

Roll out the dough on a floured surface to ¼ inch thick. Cut out 2 inch rounds with a cookie cutter and arrange on greased cookie sheets.

Bake for 10 minutes or until golden brown around the edges. Cool on a wire rack.

Russian Walnut Drops

MAKES ABOUT 2 DOZEN

¾ cup butter or margarine
¾ cup sugar
1½ cups all-purpose flour
⅛ teaspoon salt
¼ cup brandy
1 cup finely chopped walnuts

Preheat the oven to 350°.

Cream the butter or margarine with the sugar until light and fluffy. Sift the flour and salt into the bowl and mix well. Add the brandy, then mix in the walnuts.

Drop by heaped teaspoonfuls onto greased cookie sheets, leaving room for spreading. Bake for 20–25 minutes or until golden brown. Cool on a wire rack.

CANDIES

It's not only children who love candies — most adults will admit to a sweet-tooth. And making candies can be almost as much fun as eating them, especially when you can lick the spoon!

Candy-making is surprisingly easy. The step-by-step photographs in this section will make candying fruit, dipping chocolates and producing melt-in-the-mouth humbugs and fondants child's play. And children will certainly enjoy helping you make these and many other delicious confections. A word of warning: if sugar boiling is part of the candy-making process, adult supervision is essential.

A selection of delicious candies: (Back row) Coconut Ice (page 128); Clear Mints (page 126); Marshmallows (page 126) and Barley Sugar (page 130). Front: Candied Brazil Nuts (page 144); Yorkshire Cinder Toffee (page 173); Fondants (page 167); Nougat (page 146) and Humbugs (page 134).

Chapter One

BASIC INFORMATION

Ingredients

Sugar: For candy-making, granulated, confectioner's and brown sugar are all used as well as corn and maple syrup, molasses and honey. Use the sweetener specified in the recipe: don't substitute one for another. Corn syrup used with sugar makes a candy creamy or soft and chewy, depending on the proportions of each.

Always dissolve sugar in water over low heat, stirring frequently. The sugar must be completely dissolved and the syrup clear before it reaches boiling point, otherwise the syrup could crystallize, especially at high temperatures. While the sugar is being dissolved, brush any sugar grains back into the liquid using a damp pastry brush. Alternatively, if the recipe ingredients include butter, grease the sides of the saucepan with sweet butter to prevent the sugar grains clinging.

After the sugar syrup has come to a boil, stop stirring unless the recipe specifies otherwise. Stirring during boiling will encourage crystallization, and result in a grainy-textured candy.

When pouring the candy mixture out of the saucepan, don't scrape the pan: there may be sugar crystals on the side.

Cream of tartar: When added to boiling sugar syrup, cream of tartar will help stop the sugar crystallizing. However, it also inhibits sugar melting or dissolving, so it is usually added after the sugar has been dissolved. Lemon juice and vinegar have the same effect as cream of tartar, and may be substituted for it. Use 1 tablespoon lemon juice or vinegar for 1 teaspoon cream of tartar.

Butter: Butter adds richness and flavor to candy as well as slowing down crystallization. Always use sweet (unsalted) butter. The fat content of milk, cream, chocolate, etc. has the same effect as butter in a candy recipe.

Chocolate: Chocolate is used a lot in candy-making. Unsweetened and semisweet baker's chocolate are called for to make fudge, truffles, nougat and toffees. For dipped chocolates, use the special candy-making chocolate. This waxy chocolate coats fondants, caramels, etc., smoothly and keeps its gloss.

Unsweetened cocoa powder is also sometimes used to flavor candies, and to coat those that are sticky or creamy, such as truffles. Chocolate sprinkles are another attractive coating.

Colorings: Always use edible food coloring, and be sparing. Remember that you can add a few more drops, but you can't take any away.

Other ingredients: These include eggs, milk, condensed milk, nuts, candied and glacé fruits, flavoring extracts such as vanilla, almond and oil of peppermint, liqueurs and citrus juices.

TESTER'S TIP

Patience is a necessary virtue for candymakers. It can take between 20 and 30 minutes to dissolve 2 cups of sugar completely. So don't despair if it seems to take forever — just stay with it, keep stirring gently and make sure it doesn't boil before all the sugar has dissolved.

Utensils

Saucepans: A heavy-based saucepan will prevent the candy burning. And choose one that will hold about four times the volume of the candy mixture so that it cannot boil over. For delicate mixtures and melting chocolate, a double boiler is useful.

Spoons: Use a long-handled wooden spoon for stirring sugar syrups and candy mixtures. The long handle will prevent you burning yourself, and the wood will not conduct heat.

Pastry brush: A dampened pastry brush is useful for brushing any sugar grains from the sides of the pan back into the liquid while sugar is being dissolved.

Candy thermometer: This is an essential gadget for successful and trouble-free candy making. It clips onto the side of the pan and shows the temperature of the candy mixture on an easy-to-read dial. A candy mixture must be removed from the heat as soon as it reaches the specified temperature; overcooking will ruin it. And using the cold-water testing method described below takes a bit of time, practice and guesswork. If you plan to make candy regularly, a candy thermometer is an invaluable investment.

When you begin dissolving the sugar, place the candy thermometer in another saucepan of water and bring to a boil. (The thermometer should register 212°F when the water boils: a good test for its accuracy.) After the syrup boils, transfer the thermometer to the syrup. Do not let the bulb touch the bottom of the pan, but be sure it is covered by liquid and not just foam.

Continue boiling, watching the temperature rise (you'll have to bend over to read this at eye level). During the last few minutes of cooking, the temperature will rise rapidly, so be very alert.

On damp or rainy days, cook the candy mixture to 1–2° higher than that specified. All temperatures given in the recipes which follow this information are for sea level; if at high altitude adjust the temperatures according to the chart given on page 113.

To cool a candy mixture quickly, place the pan in another pan or bowl of ice-cold water and let cool until you can touch the bottom of the pan comfortably.

Other utensils: Besides ordinary baking pans into which candy mixtures are poured and left to set, there is a selection of specialized candy-making equipment available. This includes small decorative cutters, candy scrapers for working fondant and other soft mixtures as well as chocolate being prepared for dipping, small molds for setting fondants and other soft candies (an ice cube tray that makes small squares or balls is a successful substitute), wire dippers or dipping forks for dipping chocolates, a special wire rack for drying dipped chocolates, tiny paper bonbon cups, and fancy fluted foil cups.

Types of Candies

Basically, candies can be divided into four types: creamy candies, smooth candies, chocolate-dipped candies and confections that aren't really candies.

Creamy candies: The simplest of these is cooked fondant. Other creamy candies are soft mints, many chocolate-dipped cream centers, fudge and divinity.

Smooth candies: These may be hard or chewy. The hard ones include toffees, lollipops, pralines, brittles, and butterscotch. Some chewy candies are caramels, nougat, marshmallows and taffy.

Chocolate-dipped candies: Many candies lend themselves beautifully to a chocolate coating — fondants, caramels, nougat, toffees — as do nuts and fresh and candied fruits.

Confections: Sweetmeats that are not actually candies fall into this category: marzipan, truffles, candied and glacé fruits and peels, fondant-dipped fresh fruits and nuts, stuffed dried fruits such as dates, popcorn balls and candy apples — all are eaten in the same way as candies and provide the same sort of pleasure (and calories).

Storing Candies

Most homemade candies will keep in an airtight container in a cool, dry place for several weeks — if you can hide them from your family. Sticky and chewy candies such as caramels should first be wrapped individually in wax paper. Candies will also freeze well.

Temperatures and Tests for Candies

Temperatures (at sea level)	Temperatures (at 5,000 ft.)	Stage	Cold-water test*
230°–234°F	220°–224°F	thread	Syrup dropped from spoon spins 2 inch thread
234°–240°F	224°–230°F	soft ball	Syrup can be shaped into a ball but flattens when removed from water
244°–248°F	232°–238°F	firm ball	Syrup can be shaped into a firm ball which does not flatten when removed from water
250°–266°F	240°–258°F	hard ball	Syrup forms hard but pliable ball
270°–290°F	260°–280°F	soft crack	Syrup separates into threads that are not brittle
300°–310°F	290°–300°F	hard crack	Syrup separates into hard, brittle threads

*To make a cold-water test, remove the saucepan containing the candy mixture from the heat. Drop a little of the syrup into a small bowl of very cold (but not ice cold) water, then check the stage it has reached according to the descriptions above.

TESTER'S TIP

The illustrations on the right help you test what stage sugar has reached without a thermometer. (Top left) *thread:* dip two spoons into the syrup then separate; a thread should form that breaks at a short distance. (Top right) *soft and hard ball:* drop a little syrup into cold water, then remove and roll with your fingers into a ball, soft or hard. (Bottom left) *soft crack:* drop a little syrup into cold water; it should separate into pieces that are hard but not brittle. (Bottom right) *hard crack:* when the sugar reaches this stage, a drop put into cold water should separate into hard brittle strands.

Making Candied Cherries Step by Step

1. Wash 1 lb of cherries and remove the pits. Place the cherries in a saucepan and cover with boiling water. Cook for about 4 minutes or until tender. Drain well, reserving 1¼ cups of the liquid. Spread out the cherries, in one layer, in a heatproof dish.

2. Pour the reserved liquid back into the saucepan and add ¾ cup of sugar. Heat gently, stirring to dissolve the sugar. Add a few drops of food coloring, then bring to a boil.

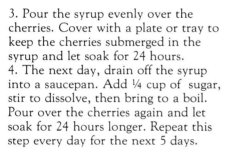

3. Pour the syrup evenly over the cherries. Cover with a plate or tray to keep the cherries submerged in the syrup and let soak for 24 hours.

4. The next day, drain off the syrup into a saucepan. Add ¼ cup of sugar, stir to dissolve, then bring to a boil. Pour over the cherries again and let soak for 24 hours longer. Repeat this step every day for the next 5 days.

5. The next day drain off the syrup into a saucepan. Add 6 tablespoons of sugar, stir to dissolve and bring to a boil. Remove from the heat and stir in the cherries.

6. Return the pan to the heat and simmer for 3–4 minutes. Pour the cherries and syrup back into the dish, cover and let soak for 48 hours.

7. On the tenth day, repeat steps 5 and 6 but let soak for 4 days instead of 48 hours. The syrup should be like clear honey.

8. Drain off the syrup. Place the fruit on a wire rack over a cookie sheet.

9. Dry the cherries in a warm place or in a 250°F oven until they no longer feel sticky.

10. For a glacé finish, place 2 cups sugar and ⅔ cup of cold water in a saucepan and heat gently, stirring to dissolve the sugar. Bring to a boil and boil for 2 minutes. Remove from the heat and keep warm.

11. Have a saucepan of boiling water ready. Pour some of the sugar syrup into a cup. Dip the cherries, one at a time, first into the boiling water and then into the syrup. When the syrup in the cup becomes cloudy, discard and replace with fresh syrup. As the cherries are dipped in the syrup, arrange them on a wire rack over a cookie sheet.

12. Dry the cherries as in step 9. Place in paper bonbon cups.

VARIATION: For a crystallized finish, dip the cherries, one at a time, into the boiling water, then coat quickly with granulated sugar.

Chapter Two

CANDY FAVORITES

Popcorn Balls

MAKES 8–10

1 cup sugar
¾ cup water
¼ teaspoon salt
¼ cup light corn syrup
½ teaspoon vinegar
½ teaspoon vanilla
10 cups popped corn

Place the sugar, water, salt, syrup and vinegar in a heavy-based saucepan. Heat, stirring to dissolve the sugar. Bring to a boil and boil until the mixture reaches 250–266° on a candy thermometer. Stir in the vanilla.

Place the corn in a large bowl. Gradually pour the syrup over the corn, folding gently just to mix. Shape into balls with buttered hands. Let set.

Salt Water Taffy

MAKES ABOUT 5 DOZEN

2 cups sugar
1 cup light corn syrup
1½ teaspoons salt
1 cup water
2 tablespoons sweet butter
¼ teaspoon oil of peppermint
few drops of green food coloring

Place the sugar, syrup, salt, water and butter in a heavy-based saucepan. Heat, stirring to dissolve the sugar. Bring to a boil and boil until the mixture reaches 250–266° on a candy thermometer.

Remove from the heat and stir in the oil of peppermint and food coloring. Pour onto a greased heatproof surface or cookie sheet. Leave until cool enough to handle.

With oiled hands, gather the mixture into a ball and pull to make a rope about 20 inches long. Fold in half and pull out again. Continue pulling until the taffy is light in color.

Cut it into four portions and pull each into a rope about ½ inch thick. Cut into bite-size pieces with oiled scissors. Wrap each piece in wax paper.

Vanilla Fudge

MAKES 64

2 cups sugar
⅔ cup evaporated milk
4 tablespoons sweet butter
⅔ cup milk
½ teaspoon vanilla

Place the sugar, evaporated milk, butter and milk in a heavy-based saucepan. Heat, stirring until melted and smooth. Bring to a boil and boil until the mixture reaches 234–240° on a candy thermometer.

Stir in the vanilla. Pour into a greased 8 inch square pan. Let set, then cut into 1 inch squares.

Brown Sugar Fudge

MAKES 64

1 cup evaporated milk
¼ cup water
2⅔ cups firmly packed brown sugar
4 tablespoons sweet butter
½ teaspoon vanilla

Place the milk, water and sugar in a heavy-based saucepan and heat, stirring until melted and smooth. Add the butter, in small pieces, and stir until melted.

Bring to a boil and boil, stirring occasionally, until the mixture reaches 234–240° on a candy thermometer.

Reduce the heat and stir in the vanilla. Cook, stirring, until the mixture begins to form grains. Pour into a greased 8 inch square pan. Let harden slightly before marking into 1 inch squares. Leave in the pan until completely set.

Chocolate Nut Fudge

MAKES 64

2 cups sugar
¾ cup milk
2 squares (1 oz each) semisweet
   chocolate
4 tablespoons sweet butter
½–¾ cup chopped walnuts

Place the sugar, milk and chocolate in a heavy-based saucepan and heat, stirring until melted and smooth. Bring to a boil and boil, without stirring, until the mixture reaches 234–240° on a candy thermometer. Remove from the heat and let cool for 5 minutes.

Gradually stir in the butter, in small pieces, until melted and the fudge mixture is smooth. Stir in the nuts.

Pour into a greased 8 inch square pan. Let harden slightly before marking into 1 inch squares. Leave in the pan until completely set.

Chocolate Nut Fudge

Date and Honey Fudge

MAKES 64

2 cups sugar
⅔ cup water
½ cup sweet butter
¾ cup finely chopped pitted dates
¼ cup honey

Place all the ingredients in a heavy-based saucepan. Heat, stirring to dissolve the sugar. Bring to a boil and boil until the mixture reaches 234–240° on a candy thermometer.

Remove from the heat. Beat the mixture with a wooden spoon until it is the consistency of heavy cream. Pour into a greased 8 inch square pan. Mark into 1 inch squares and let cool until set.

Almond Dream Fudge

MAKES 64

2 cups sugar
4 tablespoons sweet butter
¾ cup heavy cream
½ cup water
1 teaspoon almond extract
1 cup sliced blanched almonds

Place the sugar, butter, cream and water in a heavy-based saucepan. Heat until melted and smooth. Bring to a boil and boil until the mixture reaches 234–240° on a candy thermometer.

Stir in the almond extract and continue stirring until the mixture becomes grainy. Remove from the heat and stir in the sliced almonds.

Pour into a greased 8 inch square pan. Let cool until almost set, then cut into 1 inch squares. Leave to cool completely in the pan.

Filbert Toffee

MAKES 64

½ cup sweet butter
¾ cup chopped blanched filberts
1⅓ cups firmly packed brown sugar
½ cup light corn syrup
1 teaspoon vanilla

Place all the ingredients in a heavy-based saucepan. Heat, stirring to dissolve the sugar. Bring to a boil and boil until the mixture reaches 270–290° on a candy thermometer. Do not let the mixture brown.

Pour into a greased 8 inch square pan. Let cool until almost set, then mark into 1 inch squares. Leave in the pan until completely cold.

Honeycomb Toffee

MAKES ABOUT 10 DOZEN

2 cups sugar
¾ cup water
⅛ teaspoon cream of tartar
½ cup light corn syrup or honey
1 teaspoon baking soda

Place the sugar, all but 2 tablespoons of the water, the cream of tartar and syrup or honey in a heavy-based saucepan. Heat, stirring to dissolve the sugar. Bring to a boil and boil, without stirring, until the mixture reaches 300–310° on a candy thermometer.

Remove from the heat. Dissolve the soda in the remaining water and stir into the toffee mixture. Continue stirring until the mixture swells up, then pour into two greased 8×12 inch pans.

Let cool until half set, then mark into squares with an oiled knife. Leave to cool completely in the pans.

Butterscotch

MAKES ABOUT 3 DOZEN

2 cups sugar
1¼ cups water
¼ teaspoon cream of tartar
6 tablespoons sweet butter
¼ teaspoon vanilla

Place the sugar and water in a heavy-based saucepan and heat, stirring to dissolve the sugar. Stir in the cream of tartar. Bring to a boil and boil, without stirring, until the mixture reaches 234–240° on a candy thermometer.

Remove from the heat and stir in the butter, a small piece at a time, until melted.

Return to the heat and boil to 270–290°, without stirring. Add the vanilla a drop at a time and boil to 300–310°.

Pour into a greased 8 inch square pan. Mark into oblongs and let set.

Butterscotch

Chocolate Fudge

MAKES 64

1 cup sugar
2 squares (1 oz each) unsweetened
chocolate
6 tablespoons milk
2 tablespoons sweet butter
½ teaspoon vanilla

Place the sugar, chocolate and milk in a heavy-based saucepan and heat, stirring until melted and smooth. Bring to a boil and boil, without stirring, until the mixture reaches 234–240° on a candy thermometer.

Remove from the heat and let cool for 5 minutes. Gradually stir in the butter, in small pieces, until melted and the mixture is smooth. Let cool for 30 minutes.

Add the vanilla and beat well. Pour into a greased 8 inch square pan. Let harden slightly before marking into 1 inch squares. Leave in the pan until completely set.

Chocolate Fudge and Molasses Toffee (page 124)

Molasses Toffee

MAKES 3 DOZEN

⅔ cup firmly packed brown sugar
½ cup molasses
4 tablespoons sweet butter
2 tablespoons water
pinch of cream of tartar

Place the sugar, molasses and butter in a heavy-based saucepan. Stir in the water. Heat, stirring until melted and smooth.

Bring to a boil. Stir in the cream of tartar, then boil, stirring occasionally, until the mixture reaches 250–266° on a candy thermometer.

Pour into a greased 6 inch square pan. Let harden slightly before marking into 1 inch squares. Leave in the pan until completely set.

Pecan Penuche

MAKES 64

1½ cups granulated sugar
1 cup firmly packed brown sugar
⅓ cup light cream
⅓ cup milk
2 tablespoons sweet butter
1 teaspoon vanilla
½ cup chopped pecans

Place the sugars, cream, milk and butter in a heavy-based saucepan. Heat until melted and smooth. Bring to a boil and boil until the mixture reaches 234–240° on a candy thermometer. Remove from the heat and let cool for 5 minutes.

Add the vanilla and beat until the mixture becomes very thick and starts to lose its gloss. Stir in the pecans.

Pour into a greased 8 inch square pan and spread out evenly. Mark into 1 inch squares and let cool and set.

Maple Butterscotch

MAKES 64

1⅔ cups firmly packed brown sugar
¾ cup maple syrup
½ cup sweet butter
½ cup water

Place all the ingredients in a heavy-based saucepan. Heat until melted and smooth. Bring to a boil and boil until the mixture reaches 270–290° on a candy thermometer.

Pour into a greased 8 inch square pan. Let cool until slightly set, then mark into 1 inch squares with an oiled knife. Leave to cool completely in the pan.

Divinity

MAKES ABOUT 3½ DOZEN

2½ cups sugar
½ cup light corn syrup
½ teaspoon salt
½ cup water
2 egg whites
1 teaspoon vanilla

Place the sugar, syrup, salt and water in a heavy-based saucepan. Heat, stirring to dissolve the sugar. Bring to a boil and boil, without stirring, until the mixture reaches 250–266° on a candy thermometer.

Meanwhile, beat the egg whites until stiff.

Gradually add the sugar syrup to the egg whites, beating constantly. Add the vanilla and continue beating until the mixture will hold its shape.

Drop by teaspoonfuls onto wax paper. Let set.

Clear Mints

MAKES ABOUT 5 DOZEN

2 cups sugar
¾ cup water
¾ cup light corn syrup
few drops of blue food coloring
10 drops of oil of peppermint

Place the sugar and water in a heavy-based saucepan. Heat, stirring to dissolve the sugar. Bring to a boil. Stir in the corn syrup, then boil until the mixture reaches 300–310° on a candy thermometer.

Reduce the heat to low and cook for a further 3 minutes. Stir in the food coloring and oil of peppermint.

Pour into a greased 12×8 inch pan. Let harden slightly before marking into oblongs. Leave in the pan until completely set.

Marshmallows

MAKES ABOUT 5 DOZEN

2 cups granulated sugar
3 tablespoons light corn syrup
1¼ cups water
2 envelopes (2 tablespoons) unflavored gelatin
2 egg whites
¼ teaspoon vanilla
1 tablespoon cornstarch
2 tablespoons confectioner's sugar

Place the granulated sugar, syrup and ⅔ cup of the water in a heavy-based saucepan. Heat, stirring to dissolve the sugar. Bring to a boil and boil until the mixture reaches 250–266° on a candy thermometer.

Meanwhile, dissolve the gelatin in the remaining water.

Remove the sugar syrup from the heat and stir in the gelatin mixture. Beat the egg whites until stiff, then gradually beat in the hot syrup mixture. Stir in the vanilla. Continue beating until the mixture is thick.

Pour into a greased 9 inch square pan. Let set at room temperature for 24 hours, then cut into squares. Mix the cornstarch with the confectioner's sugar. Coat the marshmallows with this mixture.

Variations: If desired, add a few drops of red food coloring with the vanilla to make pink marshmallows. The marshmallows may be coated with shredded coconut instead of cornstarch and confectioner's sugar.

A selection of favorite candies (clockwise from the top): Nougat (page 146); Russian Caramels (page 128); Barley Sugar (page 130); Peppermint-flavored Coconut Ice (page 128); Pink-tinted Marshmallows (page 126); Heart-shaped Fondants (page 167); Clear Mints (page 126); Coconut Ice (page 128) and Quick Chocolate Fudge (page 152).

Russian Caramels

MAKES 64

¾ cup granulated sugar
⅓ cup firmly packed light brown sugar
3 tablespoons light corn syrup
6 tablespoons sweet butter
¼ cup water
3 tablespoons evaporated milk
¼ teaspoon vanilla

Place the sugars, syrup, 2 tablespoons of the butter and the water in a heavy-based saucepan. Heat until melted and smooth. Bring to a boil and boil until the mixture reaches 234–240° on a candy thermometer.

Stir in the evaporated milk and the rest of the butter. Boil to 250–266°, stirring occasionally.

Remove from the heat and stir in the vanilla. Pour into a greased 8 inch square pan. Let set, then cut into 1 inch squares.

Coconut Ice

MAKES 64

2 cups sugar
⅔ cup milk
1⅓ cups shredded coconut
red food coloring

Place the sugar and milk in a heavy-based saucepan. Heat, stirring to dissolve the sugar. Bring to a boil and boil until the mixture reaches 234–240° on a candy thermometer.

Remove from the heat and stir in the coconut. Pour half the mixture into a greased 8 inch square pan and spread out over the bottom.

Add a few drops of red food coloring to the remaining mixture to tint it pink. Pour over the top of the white mixture and press down firmly. Let set in the pan, then cut into 1 inch squares to serve.

Variation: Tint the top layer green and flavor it with a few drops of oil of peppermint.

Coffee Walnut Fudge

MAKES 64

1 cup light cream
¼ cup strong black coffee
2⅔ cups firmly packed brown sugar
4 tablespoons sweet butter
¾ cup chopped walnuts

Place the cream, coffee and sugar in a heavy-based saucepan and heat, stirring to dissolve the sugar. Stir in the butter, in small pieces. When the butter has melted, bring to a boil. Boil until the mixture reaches 234–240° on a candy thermometer.

Reduce the heat to low and stir in the walnuts. Cook, stirring, until the mixture begins to become grainy.

Pour into a greased 8 inch square pan. Let cool until half set, then mark into 1 inch squares. Refrigerate until set.

Pralines

MAKES ¾ LB

¾ cup sugar
6 tablespoons water
1½ cups blanched almonds, toasted

Place the sugar and water in a heavy-based saucepan and heat, stirring to dissolve the sugar. Bring to a boil and boil until the syrup has turned a deep golden caramel (about 240° on a candy thermometer). Stir in the almonds.

Pour onto an oiled heatproof surface or cookie sheet. Let set for about 30 minutes.

Break up the praline into small pieces.

Barley Sugar

MAKES ABOUT 3 DOZEN

2 cups sugar
1¼ cups water
pinch of cream of tartar
few drops of lemon flavoring

Place the sugar, water and cream of tartar in a heavy-based saucepan. Heat, stirring to dissolve the sugar. Bring to a boil and boil, without stirring, until the mixture reaches 300–310° on a candy thermometer. It will be pale amber in color.

Remove from the heat and stir in the lemon flavoring. Pour onto an oiled heatproof work surface and let cool for 5 minutes.

Fold the sides of the mixture into the middle to make a long, fairly straight strip. Cut pieces off the strip with oiled kitchen scissors and twist to make corkscrews. Let cool completely.

If desired, the twisted strips may be curved into cane shapes.

Nut Brittle Suckers

MAKES ABOUT 12

1 cup sugar
3 tablespoons light corn syrup
½ cup water
1 tablespoon sweet butter
½ cup chopped blanched almonds or unroasted peanuts
½ teaspoon lemon flavoring
1 teaspoon baking soda

Place the sugar, syrup and water in a heavy-based saucepan and heat, stirring to dissolve the sugar. Bring to a boil and boil, without stirring, until the mixture reaches 300–310° on a candy thermometer.

Gently stir in the butter and almonds or peanuts and boil until the nuts begin to brown. Remove from the heat. Sprinkle the lemon flavoring and baking soda on top, then stir well, allowing the mixture to foam up in the pan.

Arrange wooden popsicle sticks on an oiled cookie sheet. Spoon the almond mixture thinly over one end of each stick. Let cool until set.

Barley Sugar

Nut Brittle Suckers and Barley
Sugar shaped into Canes

Caramels

MAKES 64

1⅓ cups firmly packed brown sugar
3 tablespoons water
½ cup sweet butter
3 tablespoons light cream
½ teaspoon vanilla

Place the sugar and water in a heavy-based saucepan. Heat, stirring to dissolve the sugar. Stir in the remaining ingredients. Bring to a boil and boil, without stirring, until the mixture reaches 250° on a candy thermometer.

Pour into a greased 8 inch square pan. Let cool until set, then cut into 1 inch squares.

Uncooked Coconut Fondant Balls

MAKES ABOUT 4 DOZEN

4 cups confectioner's sugar
6 tablespoons condensed milk
½ teaspoon vanilla
½ cup toasted shredded coconut

Sift the sugar into a bowl. Add the condensed milk and vanilla and mix until smooth.

Place the fondant on a surface sprinkled with confectioner's sugar and knead until soft and pliable. Cover and let rest for 2 hours.

Roll the fondant into small balls and coat with the coconut.

Variations: The fondant may be flavored with almond extract, oil of peppermint, etc., and colored with a few drops of food coloring. Instead of coconut, the fondant balls may be coated with chocolate sprinkles, grated chocolate, chopped nuts, etc. If desired, the fondant may be rolled out to 1 inch thick and cut into various decorative shapes with small cookie or petits fours cutters.

Fudge-coated Tangerines

MAKES ABOUT 5 DOZEN

2 cups sugar
1 tablespoon sweet butter
5 tablespoons evaporated milk
1 cup milk
few drops of vanilla
5 tangerines, peeled and
   segmented

Place the sugar, butter and milks in a heavy-based saucepan. Heat until melted and smooth. Bring to a boil and boil until the mixture reaches 234–240° on a candy thermometer.

Remove from the heat, add the vanilla and beat for 1 minute. Dip the tangerine segments quickly into the fudge, using a fork or wooden pick. Place them on wax paper and let set.

Note: Be sure all white pith has been removed from the tangerine segments.

Orange or Lemon Gum Drops

MAKES ABOUT 3 DOZEN

⅔ cup orange or lemon juice
½ cup glycerine
2 envelopes (2 tablespoons)
   unflavored gelatin
2 tablespoons sugar

Place the orange or lemon juice, glycerine and gelatin in the top of a double boiler. Heat, stirring, until the gelatin has dissolved. Pour onto a plate or into a layer cake pan. Let cool and set.

Cut into squares with oiled scissors and coat with the sugar.

Note: If using orange juice, add 1–2 teaspoons of lemon juice for sharper flavor.

Striped Humbugs Step by Step

MAKES ABOUT 5 DOZEN

**2²/₃ cups firmly packed brown
  sugar**
4 tablespoons sweet butter
1¼ cups water
pinch of cream of tartar
5 drops of oil of peppermint

1. Place all the ingredients in a heavy-based saucepan and heat until melted and smooth. Bring to a boil and boil until the mixture reaches 270–290° on a candy thermometer.

2. Let cool for 5 minutes. Brush a heatproof work surface with oil.

3. When the mixture has cooled enough to thicken, pour onto the oiled work surface.

4. Leave until cool enough to handle. Oil your hands liberally.

5. Gather up the mixture and twist to make a rope about 20 inches long. Fold in half and pull out again.

6. Continue twisting and pulling until the mixture is elastic and shiny. Divide it in half.

7. Form one portion into a ball. Pull out into a rope about 1 inch thick and set aside.

8. Work the other portion by pulling and twisting until it is paler than the rope. Pull this portion into a rope.

9. Twist the ropes together and form into a ball. Cut in half with an oiled sharp knife.

10. Twist into two ropes. Cut off 1 inch pieces with an oiled pair of kitchen scissors. Half twist the pieces and cut again to give the traditional shape.

11. Let cool until set, then store in an airtight container.

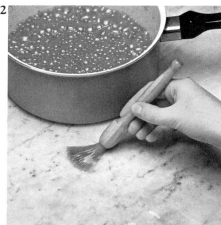

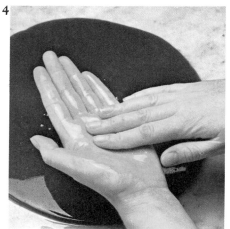

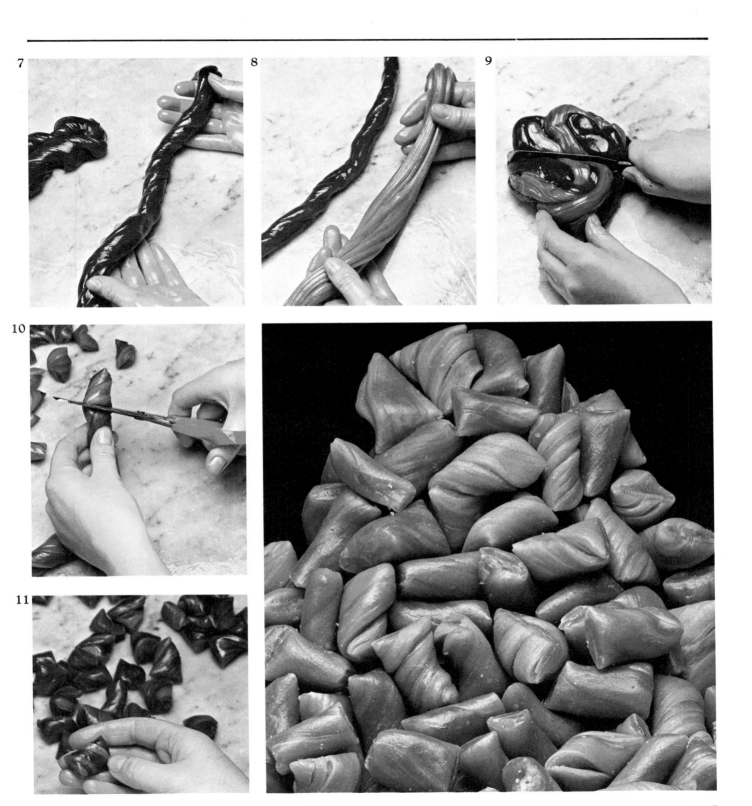

Lemon Pastilles

MAKES ABOUT 2 DOZEN

¾ cup granulated sugar
½ cup confectioner's sugar
¾ cup water
½ teaspoon lemon flavoring
few drops of yellow food coloring

Place the sugars and water in a heavy-based saucepan. Heat, stirring to dissolve the sugars. Stir in the lemon flavoring and food coloring. Bring to a boil and boil until the mixture reaches 250–266° on a candy thermometer.

Remove from the heat and let cool for 3 minutes.

Drop by teaspoonfuls (using an oiled teaspoon) onto an oiled heatproof surface or cookie sheets. Let cool and harden.

Uncooked Mocha Fudge

MAKES ABOUT 3 DOZEN

1 pkg (3 oz) cream cheese
2½ cups confectioner's sugar
2 squares (1 oz each) semisweet
  chocolate, melted
1–2 tablespoons strong black coffee

Beat the cream cheese until light and fluffy. Gradually beat in the sugar. Beat in the chocolate and coffee.

Press the mixture into a greased 6 inch square pan and spread out evenly. Refrigerate until set. Cut into 1 inch squares to serve.

Nut Clusters

MAKES ABOUT 3 DOZEN

2 cups roasted unsalted peanuts
¾ cup unblanched filberts
¾ cup chopped unblanched almonds
2 cups sugar

Combine the nuts. Place the sugar in a heavy-based saucepan and melt over low heat until the syrup turns deep golden brown. Stir in the nut mixture and remove the saucepan from the heat.

Drop by teaspoonfuls (using an oiled teaspoon) onto greased cookie sheets. Let cool and harden.

Walnut Rum Caramels

MAKES 64

¾ cup milk
4 cups granulated sugar
¼ cup light corn syrup
4 tablespoons sweet butter
1 cup chopped walnuts
2 teaspoons dark rum

Place the milk and sugar in a heavy-based saucepan. Heat, stirring to dissolve the sugar. Stir in the syrup and butter until melted and smooth. Bring to a boil and boil until the mixture reaches 250–266° on a candy thermometer.

Stir in the chopped walnuts and rum and cook for a further 1 minute.

Pour into a greased 8 inch square pan. Let cool until half set, then mark into 1 inch squares. Leave to cool completely in the pan.

Honey and Walnut Candies

MAKES ABOUT 5 DOZEN

2 cups honey
⅓ cup firmly packed brown sugar
grated rind and juice of 1 lemon
2 cups chopped walnuts

Place the honey, sugar and lemon rind and juice in a heavy-based saucepan. Heat, stirring to dissolve the sugar. Bring to a boil and boil until the mixture reaches 244–248° on a candy thermometer.

Meanwhile, toast the walnuts under the broiler.

Stir the walnuts into the syrup. Pour into a greased 8 inch square pan. Let cool until set, then cut into 1 inch squares with a knife dipped in hot water.

Candy Apples

MAKES 10

2⅔ cups firmly packed brown sugar
4 tablespoons sweet butter
2 teaspoons malt vinegar
⅔ cup water
2 tablespoons light corn syrup
10 crisp apples

Place the sugar, butter, vinegar, water and syrup in a large heavy-based saucepan. Heat until melted and smooth. Bring to a boil and boil until the mixture reaches 300–310° on a candy thermometer. Remove from the heat.

Pierce the apples with wooden sticks and dip them into the hot candy mixture, tipping the saucepan if necessary. When the apples are well coated, place them on wax paper and let cool and harden.

Candy Apples

Chapter Three

CANDY CLASSICS

Marzipan Filberts

1 cup ground almonds
¾ cup confectioner's sugar
2 tablespoons granulated sugar
½ egg yolk
few drops of almond extract
½ cup chopped blanched filberts
1 egg white, beaten until frothy
2 drops of red food coloring
24 blanched filberts, toasted

Mix together the almonds, sugars, egg yolk and almond extract to make a paste. Place on a work surface sprinkled with confectioner's sugar or cornstarch and knead for about 5 minutes or until very smooth.

Roll out the paste to a rectangle about ¼ inch thick. Mix the chopped filberts with the egg white and food coloring and spread over the rectangle, leaving a 1 inch border. Fold in half and then into quarters and roll out again. Repeat the folding and rolling twice.

Roll the paste into walnut-size balls and press a toasted filbert into each. Place in paper candy cups.

Nut Princesses

MAKES 2½ DOZEN

¾ cup sugar
1½ cups sliced, blanched almonds
6 squares (1 oz each) semisweet
    chocolate
1 tablespoon brandy
1 tablespoon sweet butter
MARZIPAN
3 cups ground almonds
2¼ cups confectioner's sugar
6 tablespoons granulated sugar
1–1½ egg yolks
¼ teaspoon almond extract

Place the sugar in a saucepan and melt over gentle heat. Cook until the syrup turns a rich golden brown. Stir in the almonds and cook for 1 minute, then pour the mixture onto an oiled heatproof surface or cookie sheet. Let cool and set.

Meanwhile, make the marzipan. Mix together all of the ingredients to make a paste. Place on a work surface sprinkled with confectioner's sugar or cornstarch and knead for about 5 minutes or until very smooth. Roll the marzipan into 30 small balls.

Crush the set sugar and almond mixture with a meat mallet or rolling pin to a powder.

Place the chocolate, brandy and butter in a heavy-based saucepan and melt over low heat. Remove from the heat. Dip each marzipan ball into the chocolate mixture, then coat with the sugar and nut powder.

Place the nut princesses on wax paper and let set.

Marzipan Dates

MAKES 2 DOZEN

½ cup ground almonds
¼ cup sugar
½ egg white, beaten until frothy
1 teaspoon rum or sherry
1 teaspoon almond extract
2–3 drops of red or green food
    coloring (optional)
24 pitted dates
24 walnut quarters

Mix together the almonds, sugar, egg white, rum or sherry and almond extract to make a paste. Tint with the food coloring, if desired.

Divide the marzipan into 24 portions and shape into ovals. Place in the dates. Press a walnut quarter into the marzipan and place in paper candy cups.

Peppermint Creams

MAKES ABOUT 1 LB

4 cups confectioner's sugar
1 teaspoon lemon juice
1 egg white
4 drops of oil of peppermint

Mix together all the ingredients. Roll out on a work surface sprinkled with confectioner's sugar to ¼ inch thick.

Cut out rounds or other shapes and place on foil. Let set for at least 24 hours before serving.

Variation: You can tint your peppermint creams pink or green by adding a drop or two of food coloring.

Peppermint Creams

Violet Creams

MAKES ABOUT 2 DOZEN

4 drops of purple food coloring (or a
   mixture of red and blue)
¼ teaspoon violet extract
1 lb cooked fondant (see page 167)
CRYSTALLIZED VIOLETS
½ oz gum arabic
1 tablespoon rose water
4 small posies of violets (24 flowers)
6 tablespoons sugar

First make the crystallized violets. Place the gum arabic and rose water in a screw-top jar and shake for 2–3 minutes. Let soak for 1–3 hours, shaking the jar occasionally, until the gum arabic has dissolved.

Cut the stalks from the violets, leaving ¼ inch near the flower. Holding the flowers by the stalks, paint on both sides of the petals with the gum arabic. Use a soft, fine paint brush to do this.

Dip each flower into the sugar to coat both sides. Place on wax paper and let set in a warm dry place for at least 24 hours.

Knead the food coloring and violet extract into the fondant. Roll into walnut-size pieces. Flatten slightly, then press a crystallized violet into each one. Let set for 1 hour before serving.

Violet Creams

Almond Sticks

MAKES ABOUT 7½ DOZEN

2 cups blanched almonds
1¼ cups sugar
2 egg whites
¼ cup rum

Preheat the oven to 350°.

Put all the almonds, 1 cup of the sugar, 1 egg white and the rum into a blender or food processor and work to a paste. Or pound the almonds with 1 cup of the sugar in a mortar with a pestle. Add 1 egg white and the rum and mix to a stiff paste.

Roll out the paste on a floured surface to a rectangle about ⅛ inch thick. Cut into 3 × ½ inch strips.

Lightly beat the remaining egg white until frothy. Dip the paste strips in the egg white, then coat with the remaining sugar.

Arrange the strips on a greased and floured cookie sheet. Bake for 8 minutes or until just golden and firm to the touch. Cool on the cookie sheet.

Candied Brazil Nuts

MAKES ½ LB

¼ lb shelled Brazil nuts
1 cup firmly packed brown sugar
4 tablespoons sweet butter
1 tablespoon light corn syrup
1 teaspoon malt vinegar

Preheat the oven to 250°.

Spread out the nuts on an oiled cookie sheet. Place in the oven and leave to warm.

Place the remaining ingredients in a heavy-based saucepan and heat until melted and smooth. Bring to a boil and boil until the mixture reaches 300–310° on a candy thermometer.

Pour the mixture into the top of a double boiler. Dip each nut into the toffee mixture, then place on wax paper. Let cool and set.

Caramelized Grapes

MAKES 1 LB

1 lb green or purple grapes
2 cups sugar
½ pint water
pinch of cream of tartar

Break the grapes into pairs.

Place the sugar and water in a heavy-based saucepan and heat, stirring to dissolve the sugar. Add the cream of tartar and bring to a boil. Boil until the mixture reaches 300–310° on a candy thermometer. Remove from the heat.

Dip the grapes into the syrup to coat on all sides. Place on an oiled cookie sheet and let set.

Bourbon Balls

MAKES ABOUT 3 DOZEN

2½ cups plain sweet cookie crumbs
1 cup confectioner's sugar
2 tablespoons unsweetened cocoa
1 cup chopped walnuts
8 tablespoons bourbon
confectioner's sugar to dredge

Mix together the cookie crumbs, sugar, cocoa and walnuts. Add the bourbon and bind together.

Roll the mixture into walnut-size balls and coat them with confectioner's sugar.

Nougat

MAKES ABOUT 8 DOZEN

¼ cup honey
3 egg whites
1½ cups sugar
⅔ cup water
⅛ teaspoon vanilla
¼ cup light corn syrup
3 tablespoons finely chopped candied
    cherries
3 tablespoons finely chopped candied
    angelica
1 cup chopped toasted almonds

Place the honey in the top of a double boiler and leave to melt.

Beat the egg whites until stiff. Add to the honey and beat over hot water until the mixture is thick and stiff. Remove from the heat.

Place the sugar and water in a heavy-based saucepan. Heat, stirring to dissolve the sugar. Add the vanilla and corn syrup and bring to a boil. Boil until the mixture reaches 250–266° on a candy thermometer.

Add the syrup to the honey mixture and stir well. Return the double boiler to the heat and cook, beating frequently, until the mixture reaches 244–248° on a candy thermometer. This will take about 2 hours.

Stir in the cherries, angelica and nuts. Pour into a 12×8 inch pan lined with edible rice paper. Cover with another sheet of rice paper. Place a board on top and weight this down. Let cool and set for 2 hours.

Cut into 1 inch squares to serve.

Raisin Truffles

MAKES ABOUT 1½ DOZEN

⅔ cup condensed milk
2 tablespoons unsweetened cocoa
2 tablespoons sweet butter
½ cup plain sweet cookie crumbs
⅓ cup raisins

Place the condensed milk, cocoa and butter in a saucepan and bring to a boil, stirring. Boil for 3 minutes. Remove from the heat and let cool for 20 minutes.

Add the cookie crumbs and raisins to the cocoa mixture and beat well. Let cool completely.

Roll the mixture into walnut-size balls and arrange on a serving plate.

Nougat and Chocolate Nougat (page 157)

A selection of truffles (clockwise):
Raisin Truffles, Almond Truffles
(page 149)
and Whiskey Truffles (page 148).

Whiskey Truffles

MAKES 2½ DOZEN

6 squares (1 oz each) semisweet
 chocolate
1 egg yolk
2 tablespoons sweet butter
6 tablespoons confectioner's sugar
2 tablespoons whiskey
½ cup unsweetened cocoa

Place the chocolate in a heavy-based saucepan and melt over low heat. Remove from the heat and beat in the egg yolk, butter, sugar and whiskey. Let cool, then refrigerate until the mixture is thick.

Roll the mixture into 30 bottle cork shapes and coat with the cocoa. Arrange on a serving plate.

Rum Truffles

MAKES ABOUT 2½ DOZEN

1 tablespoon instant coffee powder
2 tablespoons hot water
8 squares (1 oz each) semisweet
 chocolate
½ cup sweet butter
2 tablespoons dark rum
confectioner's sugar
chocolate sprinkles

Dissolve the instant coffee in the water. Melt the chocolate in a heavy-based saucepan over low heat. Remove from the heat and stir in the butter until melted. Add the coffee and rum and mix well. Refrigerate for 1 hour or until firm.

Coat your hands with confectioner's sugar, then roll the chocolate mixture into walnut-size balls. Coat the balls with chocolate sprinkles. Put into paper candy cups and let set.

Nut Truffles

MAKES ABOUT 1 DOZEN

4 squares (1 oz each) semisweet
    chocolate
¼ cup finely chopped blanched filberts
2 tablespoons finely chopped walnuts
½ cup confectioner's sugar
½ teaspoon vanilla
1 tablespoon light cream

Place the chocolate in a heavy-based saucepan and melt over low heat. Add the remaining ingredients and mix well. Remove the saucepan from the heat and let cool for 20 minutes or until the mixture is thick.

Roll the mixture into walnut-size balls with oiled hands. Place on a plate and refrigerate for 30 minutes or until firm before serving.

Almond Truffles

MAKES 1½ DOZEN

1 cup ground almonds
¾ cup confectioner's sugar
2 tablespoons granulated sugar
½ egg yolk
½ teaspoon almond extract
¼ cup unsweetened cocoa
2 tablespoons finely chopped blanched
    almonds
SUGAR SYRUP
6 tablespoons sugar
6 tablespoons water
½ teaspoon vanilla

First make the sugar syrup. Place the ingredients in a saucepan and heat, stirring to dissolve the sugar. Bring to a boil and boil until the syrup reaches 215° on a candy thermometer. Remove from the heat and let cool.

Mix together the ground almonds, sugars, egg yolk and almond extract. Place on a work surface sprinkled with confectioner's sugar or cornstarch and knead for about 5 minutes or until very smooth.

Add the cocoa and chopped almonds to the paste and mix well to combine thoroughly. Roll the mixture into small balls. Dip into the sugar syrup and place on foil. Let cool and set before serving.

Marzipan Fruit Step by Step

MAKES ½ LB

1. Mix together ½ cup confectioner's sugar, ¼ cup granulated sugar and ½ cup ground almonds in a mixing bowl.
2. Add ½ teaspoon lemon juice, a little almond extract and ½ egg, and mix to a paste. Place on a board sprinkled with confectioner's sugar or cornstarch and knead until very smooth.

3. Cut the paste into five portions, or more if you want to make fruits other than those suggested here.
4. Knead a few drops of food coloring into each portion — red for strawberries, yellow for bananas, green for pears and apples, orange (or yellow and red) for oranges, and purple (or red and blue) or green for grapes.

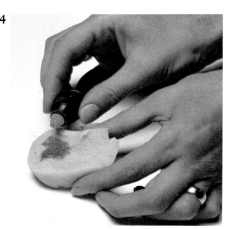

5. Break the red paste into walnut-size pieces and shape into strawberries. Roll gently on the small holes of a grater to mark the pits.
6. Stick a clove into each berry to represent the stalk. Add a few small pieces of angelica for leaves.

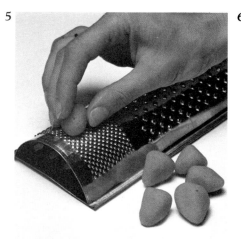

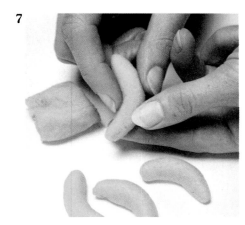

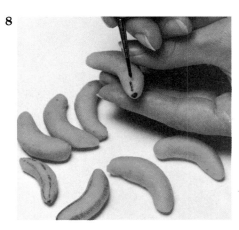

7. For bananas, shape the yellow paste into 1½ inch long sausages and curve them slightly.

8. Paint markings on the bananas with brown food coloring, using a fine paint brush.

9. For pears, mold the green paste into small pear shapes. Paint a little brown dot at the rounded end and use a clove for the stalk.

10. Use the green paste to make apples, too, with cloves for the stalk. Paint a brown dot at the flower end, and paint a rosy blush on the side with red food coloring.

11. For oranges, roll the orange paste into small balls. Roll gently over a grater to mark the skin, and add a clove to each.

12. For grapes, roll purple or green paste into tiny balls and arrange in a bunch.

Chapter Four CHOCOLATES

Quick Chocolate Fudge

MAKES 64

4 squares (1 oz each) semisweet
  chocolate
6 tablespoons sweet butter
2 tablespoons strong black coffee
¼ cup heavy cream
few drops of vanilla
4 cups confectioner's sugar

Place the chocolate, butter and coffee in a heavy-based saucepan. Heat until melted and smooth.

Remove from the heat and stir in the cream and vanilla. Gradually stir in the confectioner's sugar.

Pour into a greased 8 inch square pan and spread out evenly. Refrigerate until set, then cut into 1 inch squares to serve.

Cream Caramel Chocolates

MAKES 64

1 cup sugar
300 ml/½ pint water
½ cup light corn syrup
¾ cup condensed milk
4 tablespoons sweet butter
few drops of vanilla
1 lb candy-making chocolate

Place the sugar, water and corn syrup in a heavy-based saucepan and heat, stirring to dissolve the sugar. Bring to a boil and boil until the mixture reaches 255° on a candy thermometer.

Meanwhile, place the condensed milk and butter in another saucepan and heat until the butter has melted.

Add the butter mixture to the sugar mixture and continue boiling to 260°. Remove from the heat and dip the bottom of the pan into cold water to cool quickly. Stir in the vanilla.

Pour into a greased 8 inch square pan and let set slightly. Mark into small squares.

Prepare the chocolate for dipping (page 154). Dip in the caramels as shown in the step-by-step photographs on page 158.

Variations: Add any of the following before pouring the caramel mixture into the pan: ½ cup chopped milk or dark sweet chocolate, ½ cup chopped mixed nuts, ½ cup chopped mixed candied fruits, or ¼ cup chopped preserved stem ginger.

Chocolate Dates

MAKES ½ LB

½ lb pitted dates
30 blanched almonds (or as many as there are dates)
4 squares (1 oz each) semisweet or milk chocolate
2 drops of vanilla

Make a small slit in each date and press an almond into each date.

Melt the chocolate in a heatproof bowl over a pan of simmering water or in the top of a double boiler. Stir in the vanilla.

Dip the dates in the chocolate to coat on all sides. Tap gently on the side of the bowl to remove excess chocolate. Place on wax paper and let cool and set.

Note: If intending to keep the candies for more than 2–3 days, use candy-making chocolate.

Preparing Chocolate for Dipping Step by Step

1. Grate or cut up 1 lb candy-making chocolate. Place in a heatproof bowl over a pan of simmering water or in the top of a double boiler. Stir gently until the chocolate has melted.
2. When melted, the chocolate should register 115° on a candy thermometer. Remove from the heat.

3. Pour two-thirds of the chocolate onto a heatproof surface.
4. Stir and fold the chocolate until it cools and thickens. Do not let it set and harden.

5. Return the chocolate to the bowl or top of the double boiler. Place over the simmering water, off the heat. Stir until well mixed with the chocolate that remained in the bowl.
6. The chocolate should register 90° at this stage, and it is now ready for use.

Chocolate Kumquats

MAKES 1 DOZEN

**4 squares (1 oz each) semisweet or
dark sweet chocolate**
12 candied kumquats

Place the chocolate in a heatproof bowl over a pan of simmering water or in the top of a double boiler and melt over low heat. Remove from the heat and let cool until slightly thickened.

Dip each kumquat into the chocolate to coat on all sides. Tap gently on the side of the bowl to remove excess chocolate. Place on wax paper and let cool and set.

Note: If intending to keep the candies for more than 2–3 days, use candy-making chocolate.

Chocolate-Dipped Fruit

MAKES ½ LB

**8 squares (1 oz each) semisweet or
milk chocolate**
**½ lb mixed fruit (cherries, strawberries,
orange segments, pineapple
cubes, etc.)**

Place the chocolate in a heatproof bowl over a pan of simmering water or in the top of a double boiler. Melt until smooth.

Pat the fruit dry with paper towels, then dip into the chocolate to coat all over. Tap gently on the side of the bowl to remove excess chocolate.

Place on wax paper and let set.

Note: If intending to keep the candies for more than 2–3 days, use candy-making chocolate.

Orange Chocolate Balls

MAKES ABOUT 1½ DOZEN

6 squares (1 oz each) semisweet
  chocolate
½ cup sweet butter
3 egg yolks
3 tablespoons sugar
2 teaspoons grated orange rind
chocolate sprinkles

Place the chocolate and butter in a heavy-based saucepan and melt over low heat. Remove the saucepan from the heat and cool slightly.

Beat the egg yolks and sugar together until light and creamy. Beat in the chocolate mixture and orange rind. Refrigerate until the mixture is thick but not yet set.

Roll the mixture into walnut-size balls and coat with chocolate sprinkles. Refrigerate until set.

Chocolate Nougat

MAKES ABOUT 8 DOZEN

1 cup honey
1 cup sugar
6 tablespoons water
8 squares (1 oz each) semisweet
  chocolate
2 egg whites
3 cups blanched filberts, toasted

Place the honey in the top of a double boiler and cook, stirring frequently, for 45 minutes to 1 hour or until the honey reaches 250–266° on a candy thermometer.

Meanwhile, place ¼ cup of the sugar and ¼ cup of the water in a saucepan and heat, stirring to dissolve the sugar. Add the chocolate and cook, stirring, until it has melted. Remove from the heat and keep warm.

Place the remaining sugar and water in another saucepan and stir to dissolve the sugar. Bring to a boil and boil until the syrup turns a light nut brown. Remove from the heat.

Beat the egg whites until stiff. Gradually add the honey, beating constantly. Beat in the chocolate mixture and the caramel syrup. Stir in the filberts.

Pour the mixture into a 12×8 inch pan lined with a double thickness of edible rice paper. Using a knife dipped in cold water, spread out the nougat mixture evenly. Let cool for 20 minutes.

With the wet knife, mark the nougat into 1 inch squares. Let cool completely, before breaking into pieces to serve.

Fondant-Filled Chocolates Step by Step

1. Break 1 lb cooked fondant (page 167) into a heatproof bowl placed over a pan of simmering water or into the top of a double boiler. Heat gently until melted, then add flavoring of your choice.

2. Remove from the heat and divide the fondant into several portions. Tint each one a different color with food coloring.

3. Spoon the fondant into candy molds of differing shape. Press down well. Let set in a cool place.

4. Unmold the fondants.

5. Prepare 1 lb candy-making chocolate for dipping (page 154). Drop the fondants one at a time into the chocolate, then lift out gently. Tap gently on the side of the bowl to remove excess chocolate, then place the fondant on parchment paper.

6. If desired, gently press a crystallized violet or rose petal into the top of each chocolate.

7. For a simple decoration, press a two-pronged dipping fork on the top of the chocolate before it sets.

8. Melted milk chocolate may be piped in a squiggle or other design on top.

9. Other simple decorations include candied cherries, blanched almonds, unblanched filberts, chocolate dots, etc.

Chocolate Almond Toffees

MAKES ABOUT 3 DOZEN

2²⁄₃ cups firmly packed brown sugar
²⁄₃ cup milk
½ teaspoon almond extract
1 cup sliced blanched almonds
½ lb candy-making chocolate

Place the sugar and milk in a heavy-based saucepan. Heat, stirring to dissolve the sugar. Bring to a boil and boil until the mixture reaches 300–310° on a candy thermometer. Remove from the heat and let cool for 5 minutes.

Stir in the almond extract and almonds. Pour into a greased 6 inch square pan. Let cool until half set, then mark into 1 inch squares. Leave in the pan until cold and set.

Remove the toffee squares from the pan. Prepare the chocolate for dipping (page 154). Dip the toffee squares as shown in the step-by-step photographs on page 158.

Chocolate Peppermint Creams

MAKES ½ LB

1 egg white
4 drops of oil of peppermint
2 cups confectioner's sugar
¼ lb candy-making chocolate

Place the egg white in a bowl and beat until foamy. Add the oil of peppermint. Gradually beat in the sugar to make a stiff but still pliable paste.

Place the paste on a surface sprinkled with confectioner's sugar and knead until smooth. Roll out the paste with a sugar-dredged rolling pin to ¼ inch thick. Cut out ½ inch rounds, squares, diamonds, etc.

Prepare the chocolate for dipping (page 154). Dip in the peppermint creams as shown in the step-by-step photographs on page 158.

Variations: Use orange extract instead of oil of peppermint, and tint the mixture orange with food coloring. Sprinkle the shapes with grated orange rind and press in lightly before dipping in the chocolate.

Chocolate Eggs

MAKES ABOUT 1½ DOZEN

1½ cups plain sweet cookie crumbs
1 tablespoon unsweetened cocoa
½ cup ground almonds
2 tablespoons light corn syrup
1 tablespoon rum (optional)

Mix together all the ingredients. Take walnut-size pieces of the mixture and form into egg shapes.

Variations: Coat the eggs with shredded coconut, chopped nuts or crushed rock candy.

Rocky Road

MAKES ABOUT 4 DOZEN

7 squares (1 oz each) semisweet
   chocolate
1 tablespoon sweet butter
2 eggs
1¼ cups confectioner's sugar
½ teaspoon salt
1 teaspoon vanilla
1½ cups chopped walnuts
2 cups diced marshmallows or
   miniature marshmallows

Melt the chocolate with the butter in a heavy-based saucepan. Remove from the heat and let cool slightly.

Beat the eggs with the sugar, salt and vanilla until creamy. Beat in the chocolate mixture. Stir in the walnuts and marshmallows.

Drop by rounded teaspoonfuls onto wax paper. Refrigerate until set.

Variation: A very simple version of this can be made using 1 lb milk chocolate, either 1 cup diced marshmallows or miniature marshmallows and 1 cup chopped nuts. Melt the chocolate and pour half of it over the bottom of an 8×12 inch pan lined with wax paper. Cover with the marshmallows and nuts and pour the rest of the chocolate over the top. Let set, then break into pieces.

Chocolate Cherry Cups

MAKES 1 DOZEN

4 squares (1 oz each) semisweet
  chocolate
1 tablespoon apricot jam
12 cherries, pitted
1 square (1 oz) milk chocolate

Melt the semisweet chocolate in a heavy-based saucepan over low heat. Remove from the heat. Spoon half the chocolate into 12 small foil candy cups and turn to coat the insides evenly. Let set.

Divide the jam between the cases. Place a cherry in each cup, then cover with the remaining chocolate. Let set.

Melt the milk chocolate. Pipe a squiggle over the top of each chocolate cup. Let set.

Chocolate Nut Parasols

MAKES 6

4 squares (1 oz each) semisweet
  chocolate
1 egg
2 tablespoons sweet butter
2 teaspoons rum
½ cup chopped mixed nuts

Melt the chocolate in a heavy-based saucepan over low heat. Remove from the heat and stir in the remaining ingredients. Let cool slightly.

Meanwhile, cut out six 5 inch squares from wax paper. Roll into cone shapes and secure with tape.

Pour the chocolate mixture into the cones. Place them in a bowl of rice to keep them upright and insert a wooden stick into each. Refrigerate until set.

If desired, the wax paper may be covered with a paper doily and decorated with ribbon.

Chocolate Cherry Cups

Chocolate Nut Parasols

Chapter Five

AROUND THE WORLD CANDIES

West Indian Molasses Candies

MAKES ABOUT 2 DOZEN

1 cup molasses
2 tablespoons sugar
1½ cups shredded coconut
grated rind of 1 orange
⅛ teaspoon grated nutmeg
½ cup ground unsalted cashew nuts

Place all the ingredients in a heavy-based saucepan. Bring to a boil, stirring, then boil until the mixture reaches 230–234° on a candy thermometer.

Drop by tablespoonfuls onto dampened cookie sheets, allowing room for spreading. Let cool and set.

Greek Almond Candies

MAKES ABOUT 4 DOZEN

1 egg, separated
2 cups ground almonds (preferably freshly ground)
2 cups granulated sugar
1 tablespoon brandy
1 teaspoon ground cinnamon
2 tablespoons strong black coffee
½ cup confectioner's sugar
½ teaspoon lemon juice
1 tablespoon hot water

Preheat the oven to 400°.

Place the egg white, almonds and granulated sugar in a heavy-based saucepan. Cook over low heat for 10–12 minutes, stirring, until the mixture is very stiff and light brown.

Divide the mixture between two bowls. Add the brandy and egg yolk to one bowl, and the cinnamon and coffee to the other. Mix each well.

Spread out the brandy mixture on a cookie sheet lined with parchment paper. Cover with the coffee mixture. Bake for 5–10 minutes or until the edges are lightly browned. Remove from the oven and let cool.

Mix the confectioner's sugar with the lemon juice and water until smooth. Spread this frosting over the layered candy mixture and let set. Cut into 1 inch squares to serve.

Minted Turkish Delight

MAKES ABOUT 4 DOZEN

1½ cups granulated sugar
1 cup water
1 teaspoon lemon juice
4 envelopes (4 tablespoons) unflavored gelatin dissolved in ½ cup water
1 tablespoon crème de menthe
2 drops of green food coloring
½ cup confectioner's sugar
¼ cup cornstarch

Place the granulated sugar, water and lemon juice in a heavy-based saucepan and heat, stirring to dissolve the sugar. Bring to a boil and boil until the mixture reaches 250–266° on a candy thermometer. Remove from the heat and let cool for 10 minutes.

Add the gelatin mixture, crème de menthe and food coloring and beat well until evenly mixed. Pour into a greased 8 inch square pan and let set for 8 hours or overnight.

Sift the confectioner's sugar and cornstarch onto a work surface. Invert the Turkish Delight onto the surface and cut into 1 inch squares. Turn to coat with the sugar and cornstarch.

If not served immediately, wrap the candies in wax paper.

Cooked Fondant Step by Step

MAKES 1 LB

2 cups sugar
⅔ cup water
pinch of cream of tartar
1 tablespoon heavy cream or
  evaporated milk (optional)
coloring and flavoring

1. Place the sugar and water in a heavy-based saucepan and heat, stirring to dissolve the sugar. Add the cream of tartar and bring to a boil. Boil until the mixture reaches 234–240° on a candy thermometer.
2. Pour the syrup onto a dampened heatproof surface and let cool until a skin forms around the edges. Sprinkle over the cream or evaporated milk, if using, then work the syrup in a figure of eight movement until it is opaque and firm.
3. Scrape the mixture into a ball and knead until it is an even texture. Divide into four or more portions.
4. Add food coloring and flavoring to each portion and knead until evenly distributed.
5. For filled fondants, mold pieces of fondant around candied cherries, blanched almonds, etc.
6. For fondant shapes, roll out the fondant on a surface sprinkled with confectioner's sugar and cornstarch to about 1 inch thick. Cut out small hearts, stars, etc. with small cutters.
7. For fondant fruit, place the fondant in the top of a double boiler and melt it. Dip candied fruit such as cherries and pineapple, grapes or nuts into the fondant to coat on all sides and let set on a wire rack.
8. For molded fondants, spoon the fondant into small decorative candy molds sprinkled with cornstarch. Press down well.
9. Let set, then remove from the molds.

Spanish Almond Candies

MAKES ABOUT 2 DOZEN

1 lb blanched almonds, toasted
  (about 4 cups)
1 cup sugar
½ cup honey
MARZIPAN
1 cup ground almonds
¾ cup confectioner's sugar
2 tablespoons granulated sugar
½ egg yolk
few drops of almond extract

First make the marzipan. Mix together all the ingredients to make a paste. Place on a work surface sprinkled with confectioner's sugar or cornstarch and knead for about 5 minutes or until very smooth.

Place the almonds, sugar and honey in a heavy-based saucepan and heat, stirring to dissolve the sugar. Bring to a boil and boil for 3 minutes. Remove from the heat and stir in the marzipan until well combined.

Pour into a greased 6 inch square pan and let cool slightly. Mark into 1½ inch squares and leave in the pan to cool completely.

Russian Honey Nut Toffees

MAKES ABOUT 4 DOZEN

2 cups finely chopped walnuts
1 cup finely chopped blanched almonds
1 lb (1⅓ cups) honey
¼ cup sugar

Preheat the broiler.

Spread out the nuts in the broiler pan and broil, shaking the pan occasionally, until they are golden brown. Remove from the heat.

Place the honey and sugar in a heavy-based saucepan and heat, stirring to dissolve the sugar. Bring to a boil and boil until the mixture reaches 244–248° on a candy thermometer.

Reduce the heat to low and stir in the nuts. Cook for 10 minutes longer, stirring occasionally.

Pour into a dampened 6 inch square pan and spread out evenly. Let cool and set, then invert onto a board and cut into 1 inch squares (or other shapes).

Jewish Honey Balls

MAKES ABOUT 2 DOZEN

2 eggs
1 tablespoon ground ginger
1 tablespoon vegetable oil
2 cups all-purpose flour, sifted
1 lb (1⅓ cups) honey
1 cup sugar
1 cup chopped nuts

Lightly beat the eggs with 1 teaspoon of the ginger and the oil. Add the flour and mix to a smooth, stiff dough. Roll the dough into walnut-size balls.

Place the honey, sugar and remaining ginger in a heavy-based saucepan and heat, stirring to dissolve the sugar. Bring to a boil. Drop in the dough balls, a few at a time so the syrup does not stop boiling, and boil for 10 minutes.

Cover the pan, reduce the heat to low and continue cooking for 35–40 minutes or until the balls are golden brown. Stir occasionally, and make sure the syrup continues simmering all the time. Remove from the heat and let cool.

Coat the balls with the chopped nuts. Let set before serving.

Jewish Carrot Candies

MAKES ABOUT 1½ DOZEN

1¾ cups sugar
3 tablespoons water
1 lb carrots, grated
½ teaspoon finely chopped fresh
   ginger root
½ cup finely chopped walnuts
2 tablespoons lemon juice

Place the sugar and water in a heavy-based saucepan and heat, stirring to dissolve the sugar. Stir in the carrots and bring to a boil. Boil for 30 minutes or until the mixture is very thick.

Remove from the heat and stir in the ginger, walnuts and lemon juice. Pour into a greased 6 inch square pan. Let cool and set. Cut into 1 inch squares to serve.

French Sugared Almonds

MAKES 1 LB

2 cups sugar
½ cup water
1 teaspoon ground cinnamon
1 lb unblanched almonds

Place the sugar, water and cinnamon in a saucepan and heat, stirring to dissolve the sugar. Bring to a boil and boil until the syrup falls from a spoon in thick drops. Stir in the almonds.

Remove the pan from the heat and stir until the syrup dries into sugar.

Tip the almonds into a strainer and shake to dislodge the excess sugar. Return this sugar to the saucepan and stir in just enough water to moisten. Heat, stirring to dissolve the sugar, then bring to a boil and boil until the syrup clears.

Stir in the almonds to coat on all sides. Tip onto a greased cookie sheet and let cool and dry.

French Glazed Chestnuts

MAKES 1 LB

1 lb chestnuts
1 cup sugar
1 cup light corn syrup
⅔ cup water
1 teaspoon vanilla

Slit the chestnut skins without cutting the nuts. Place in a saucepan, cover with water and bring to a boil. Simmer for 25 minutes. Remove the chestnuts from the pan one at a time and peel off the skin.

Place the sugar, corn syrup and water in a heavy-based saucepan and heat, stirring to dissolve the sugar. Bring to a boil. Add the chestnuts and vanilla and boil for 10 minutes.

Lift out the chestnuts with a slotted spoon and arrange on a wire rack. Let drain for 24 hours. Reserve the syrup.

The next day, bring the syrup to a boil again. Add the chestnuts and simmer for 5–10 minutes or until well coated with the syrup.

Lift the chestnuts onto the wire rack and let dry.

French Glazed Chestnuts

Portuguese Fig and Nut Candies

MAKES ABOUT 2½ DOZEN

¾ lb dried figs, chopped (about 2 cups)
¾ cup chopped pitted dates
30 blanched almonds, toasted
½ cup finely chopped blanched filberts
½ cup finely chopped blanched
  almonds

Purée the figs and dates in a blender or food processor. Roll the mixture into 30 small balls. Push a toasted almond into the center of each ball and press the fig mixture around to enclose completely.

Mix the chopped filberts with the chopped almonds. Coat each ball with the nuts.

Israeli Haroset

MAKES ABOUT 5 DOZEN

3 large apples, peeled, cored and
  chopped
5 bananas, chopped
1 lb dates, pitted and chopped
  (about 3 cups)
2 cups finely chopped ground nuts
2 teaspoons ground cinnamon
2 teaspoons ground ginger
1 tablespoon grated lemon rind
1 tablespoon grated orange rind
½ cup dry red wine
2½ cups matzo meal

Place the apples, bananas, dates, groundnuts, spices and lemon and orange rind in a bowl and mash to a paste. Alternatively, purée in a blender or food processor. Stir in the wine.

Add enough matzo meal to make a stiff paste. Roll the paste into walnut-size balls and arrange on a serving plate.

Middle Eastern Almond Drops

MAKES ABOUT 1½ DOZEN

1 cup ground almonds
1¼ cups confectioner's sugar
5 tablespoons orange juice
10 pistachio nuts, skinned and halved

Mix together the almonds, 1 cup of the sugar and the orange juice to make a stiff paste. Knead until smooth, then let rest for a few minutes.

Roll the paste into walnut-size balls and coat with the remaining sugar. Press a pistachio half into the top of each ball.

Yorkshire Cinder Toffee

MAKES ABOUT ¾ LB

⅓ cup imported British golden syrup,
   or light corn syrup
¾ cup + 2 tablespoons sugar
3 tablespoons sweet butter
2 tablespoons water
½ teaspoon vinegar
1 teaspoon baking soda

Place the syrup, sugar, butter and water in a heavy-based saucepan and heat, stirring to dissolve the sugar. Bring to a boil and boil, without stirring, until the mixture reaches 300–310° on a candy thermometer.

Remove from the heat and stir in the vinegar and soda. When the mixture rises up in the pan, pour it into a greased 9 inch square pan. Let cool and set, then break into small pieces to serve.

A Log Cabin (page 176)

DECORATIVE COOKIES AND CANDIES

Any celebration — be it birthday, Easter or Christmas — is enhanced by the addition of some extra special, decorative cookies and candies. And they're almost as much fun to bake as they are to look at and eat!

Castles, log cabins, Christmas decorations, chocolate eggs and marzipan animals are surprisingly easy to put together, and can provide endless hours of family fun as everyone helps to get the festivities off to a good and early start.

A Log Cabin

2 chocolate or gingerbread
   cakes baked in 9 x 5 x 3 inch pans
jam
wooden board or thick cardboard for
   base
confectioner's sugar
plain sweet rectangular cookies
1 chocolate rectangular cookie
chocolate finger cookies
assortment of brightly colored candies
2 suckers

Spread one of the cakes with a little jam, then stand in the center of a wooden board or piece of thick cardboard, as below.

Cut the second cake with a sharp knife as shown in the diagram below. Place this on top of the jam-covered cake to form the roof of the house.

Make a stiff mixture of confectioner's sugar and water to use as a paste for sticking on the candies and cookies. Cover the roof cake with plain sweet cookies and use a chocolate cookie for the door. Stick chocolate finger cookies at the corners of the walls.

Use a square of fudge for the chimney, and flat rectangles of fudge for windows. Make a ridge on the roof with jelly beans, and surround the windows with licorice candies.

Decorate the walls of the house with brightly colored candies, and arrange more candies on the board around the house to represent a path to the front door, a fence with a gate, grass, flowers, trees (the two suckers), a pond and a pile of logs.

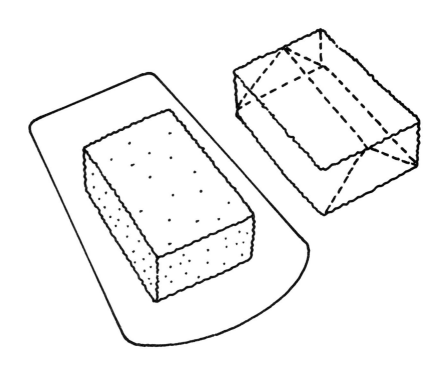

Gingerbread Castle

1 egg
1 tablespoon molasses
1 cup sugar
2 teaspoons ground cinnamon
2 teaspoons ground cardamom
½ teaspoon ground mace
1 cup butter or margarine, melted
2¾ cups all-purpose flour
1½ teaspoons baking powder
confectioner's sugar

Place the egg, molasses, sugar and spices in a bowl and beat well together. Stir in the butter or margarine. Sift the flour and baking powder into the bowl and mix to a smooth dough. Refrigerate for 30 minutes.

Preheat the oven to 325°. Knead the dough lightly. If it seems too dry, add a little more beaten egg: if too much flour has been used in the dough, the decorations will not stick to the house during baking. If too little flour has been used, the decorations will flatten out. Roll out the dough on a lightly floured surface to about ¾ inch thick.

Cut out the desired shapes of the four walls from stiff cardboard and use these as templates to cut the dough. A round-bladed kitchen knife is best for this job as it cuts the dough without tearing.

Place the four walls on cookie sheets. Roll the remaining dough into decorations for the walls: to represent doors, window frames, roof tiles, or just ornamental designs. Press them onto the dough walls.

Bake the walls one at a time for 15–20 minutes or until lightly browned. If the walls have bulged during baking, trim them straight with a sharp knife as soon as they are removed from the oven. Let cool on the cookie sheet for 5 minutes, then carefully remove the walls to a wire rack and let cool completely.

To assemble the house, make a thick mixture of confectioner's sugar and water and use it to stick the walls together. Use a wooden board or thick cardboard for the floor of the house. It may be necessary to use cardboard backing for the walls, too.

Ornamental designs can be made by hand-rolling tiny bits of dough and pressing them onto the wall before cooking.

Dough decorations flatten out if too little flour is used.

Decorations stay neatly in position when dough balance is correct.

Decorations do not adhere if too much flour has been used.

Close-up of back wall of Gingerbread Castle (page 177).

Right: Gingerbread Cabin in the Snow (page 180).

Gingerbread Cabin in the Snow

To make a cabin in the snow, use double the quantity of gingerbread dough used for Gingerbread Castle (page 177). Cut out the patterns for the parts of the cabin and the trees from cardboard, following the various diagrams given on this page. Roll out the dough and cut out each cabin shape twice and each tree shape 12 times. Bake and cool as above.

Make a paste for sticking together the parts of the house, and to represent snow, by beating 6 egg whites until stiff and folding in 6 cups confectioner's sugar.

Stick the gingerbread parts to their cardboard patterns using the paste. (The cardboard will make the house more sturdy.) Pipe the paste around the windows on the wrong side, then stick on pieces of plastic wrap to represent windows.

Stick the side and end walls firmly onto a base of wood or thick cardboard with the paste, and pipe the paste onto the inside and outside of the corners of the house. Let dry for 1 hour.

Pipe the paste thickly onto the eaves and upper parts of the side walls, then lay on the roof pieces. Press down gently and hold in place for a few minutes. Stick the chimney together and fix in place with the paste. Let dry completely.

Pipe the paste thickly onto the sides and roof, then press on an assortment of nuts and candies.

Assemble the fir trees, sticking them together with paste. Let dry, then stick to the wooden base with a blob of paste. Sprinkle the trees with confectioner's sugar.

Sprinkle the wooden base with confectioner's sugar.

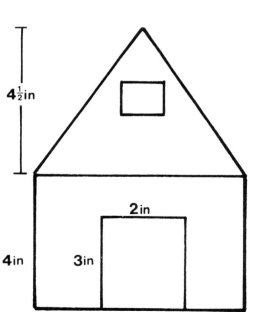

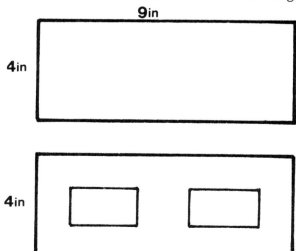

Ornamental Painted Cookies

½ cup margarine, softened
6 tablespoons butter, softened
½ cup confectioner's sugar, sifted
1¼ cups all-purpose flour
1 cup self-rising flour
1 tablespoon cornstarch
food colorings
FROSTING
1 egg white
1½–2 cups confectioner's sugar, sifted
lemon juice (if required)

Beat the margarine and butter together until well combined, then gradually beat in the sugar. Sift the flours and cornstarch into the bowl and mix to a smooth dough. Refrigerate for 30 minutes.

Preheat the oven to 350°.

Roll out the dough on a lightly floured surface to ¼ inch thick. Cut out shapes using decorative cutters 3–4 inches wide, or cut out shapes freehand or using a cardboard template as a guide. Make hearts, stars, rounds, squares, rounds with scalloped edges, signs of the zodiac, holly leaves, etc.

For cookies with a raised design, roll out two-thirds of the dough to ¼ inch thick and cut out the basic cookie shapes. Roll out the remaining dough slightly thinner and cut out the relief decorations. Press these firmly into position on the basic cookie shapes.

Arrange the cookies on cookie sheets. If the cookies are to be hung as decorations on a Christmas tree, for example, make a hole (or holes) with a metal meat skewer. Ribbon or string can be threaded through this later.

Bake for 15 minutes or until the cookies are lightly browned. Let cool on the cookie sheets for 1 minute, then remove to a wire rack to cool completely.

To make the frosting, beat the egg white until frothy. Gradually beat in the sugar and continue beating until the frosting will hold a firm peak. If necessary, stir in enough lemon juice to make a coating consistency.

Spread a layer of frosting over the cookies and let dry for several hours or overnight. When the frosting is completely dry, paint on the finishing touches with food colorings. Let dry thoroughly before threading the cookies with different-colored ribbon or string.

Far left: Ornamental Painted Cookies (page 181). Old butter, shortbread and other special molds can be used to give the 'raised' effect, or see instructions for Gingerbread Castle (page 178).

Left: Individual cookies can be designed for specific friends and family: top, the interwoven initials of an engaged couple; a smiling sun to mark the beginning of the summer vacation and pink and blue flowers on a heart-shaped cookie.

Above: Traditionally, Ornamental Painted Cookies were used to decorate the Christmas tree.

Nutty Apricot "Eggs"

MAKES 25–30

⅔ cup very finely chopped dried
    apricots
½ cup finely chopped mixed nuts
½ cup ground almonds
½ lb marzipan (see page 150)
confectioner's sugar
⅓ cup shredded coconut
red food coloring
melted chocolate to decorate

Mix the apricots with the nuts, ground almonds and marzipan. Coat your hands with confectioner's sugar, then form the mixture into 25–30 egg shapes.

Divide the coconut in half and tint one half pink with food coloring. Coat half the eggs with the pink coconut and half with the white coconut.

Drizzle a little melted chocolate over the eggs and let set.

Sugar Mice

MAKES 12

4 cups confectioner's sugar
1 large egg white
¼ cup light corn syrup
red food coloring (optional)
string
24 silver balls

Sift the sugar into a bowl. Add the egg white, syrup and a few drops of food coloring if you want to make pink mice. Mix well.

Place the paste on a surface sprinkled with confectioner's sugar and knead until smooth. Divide into 12 portions.

To make a mouse, pinch a tiny bit off one portion and reserve. Form the large piece into a pear shape, bulbous at the tail end and pointed at the nose. Use the reserved bit to make two ears and press these onto the head.

Stick a 2 inch long piece of string into the rear end of the mouse for the tail, and use silver balls for the eyes.

Place the mice on a sheet of wax paper sprinkled with cornstarch and let dry for 2 hours.

Marzipan Animals

MAKES 8

yellow food coloring
1 lb marzipan (see page 150)
4 pipe cleaners
4 yellow feathers
silver balls

Add a few drops of food coloring to the marzipan to tint it yellow and knead until evenly colored. Divide into eight portions and roll each into a ball. This will make four chicks and four cats.

For a chick, pull off one-third of one of the balls, then mold the larger piece into a chick's body. Roll the smaller piece into a ball and shape one side into the beak. Press the head onto the body. Press in silver balls for eyes.

Cut the pipe cleaners into 2 inch lengths and bend in half, pulling out the ends to form feet. Push the bent end into the body, making two legs on each chick. Push a feather into the bottom of the chick for the tail. Make three more chicks in the same way.

For a cat, pull off one-quarter of one of the remaining four balls, then mold the larger piece into a cat's body. Cut down two-thirds of the way at one side of the body to form the cat's tail. Shape the small piece into the cat's head, pulling up and shaping two ears. Press the head onto the body. Press in silver balls for the eyes. Score whiskers with a knife. Make three more cats in the same way.

Let the animals dry overnight.

Variation: To make four ducks, tint half the marzipan green with food coloring. Divide into four portions. Pull off one-quarter of one portion, then mold the larger piece into a body, pulling out the tail. Shape the small piece into a head. Press the head onto the body, then press sliced almonds into the head for the beak. Score wings with the back of a knife.

Apricot "Eggs"

MAKES 12

1 lb dried apricots
½ cup sugar
1 heaping tablespoon marmalade
½ lb marzipan (see page 150)
confectioner's sugar

Process the apricots in a blender, food processor or meat grinder until reduced to a paste. Mix in the sugar and marmalade. Shape into a roll about 2 inches thick.

Roll out the marzipan on a surface sprinkled with confectioner's sugar to an oblong large enough to wrap around the apricot roll. Wrap the marzipan around the apricot roll, then cut into 12 slices. Mold each slice into an egg shape.

Decorate as desired, with chopped or whole nuts, coconut, chocolate sprinkles, small candies, etc.

Date "Eggs"

MAKES 12

½ cup chopped pistachio nuts
2 tablespoons marmalade
12 dates, pitted
½ lb marzipan (see page 150)
confectioner's sugar

Mix together the nuts and marmalade and use to stuff the dates.

Roll out the marzipan on a surface sprinkled with confectioner's sugar. Cut into 12 squares large enough to enclose a date. Place the dates on the marzipan squares and mold into egg shapes.

Decorate as desired, with chopped or whole nuts, coconut, chocolate sprinkles, small candies, etc.

A selection of festive candies (clockwise):
Chocolate Raisin "Eggs" (Page 188),
Nutty Apricot "Eggs" (page 184),
Chocolate Easter Eggs (page 188) and
Sugar Mice (page 184).

Chocolate Easter Eggs

MAKES 6

6 eggs
16 squares (1 oz each) semisweet or
  sweet cooking chocolate
small sugar flower cake decorations
candied angelica

Pierce a small hole in each end of each egg and blow out the contents. Enlarge the hole at one end to ¼ inch in diameter. Wash the shells inside and out with cold running water, then let drain.

Dry the shells with paper towels, then place a piece of tape over the smaller hole in each egg.

Place the chocolate in the top of a double boiler and melt over hot water. Spoon the chocolate into the egg shells, stopping from time to time to be sure there are no air holes. Refrigerate until set.

Very carefully crack the egg shells and peel them away. Warm any remaining chocolate until melted and use it to stick on the flowers, leaves made from candied angelica and sugar balls in decorative patterns. Let set.

Chocolate Raisin "Eggs"

MAKES 2 DOZEN

8 squares (1 oz each) sweet cooking
  chocolate
⅔ cup raisins
1 tablespoon rum (optional)
½ lb marzipan (see page 150)
1 tablespoon strong black coffee
confectioner's sugar
hot chocolate powder
chocolate sprinkles

Place 6 squares of chocolate in the top of a double boiler and melt over hot water. Remove from the heat and stir in the raisins and rum, if using. Let cool, then shape into 24 small balls. Refrigerate until firm.

Knead the marzipan with the coffee until evenly mixed. Roll out on a surface sprinkled with confectioner's sugar to about ⅛ thick. Cut out 24 rounds using a 2 inch cutter.

Wrap the marzipan rounds around the chocolate balls, shaping slightly into egg shapes.

Melt the remaining chocolate in the double boiler. Dip each ball into the chocolate to coat, then dip half into the hot chocolate powder and half into chocolate sprinkles. Let set before serving.

Colored Easter Eggs

White-shelled eggs may be colored using natural vegetable dyes or food colorings. Place the eggs in a saucepan with the prepared vegetable dye (or food coloring and water), bring to a boil and simmer for 10 minutes. Remove the eggs with a slotted spoon and pat dry with paper towels.

Natural vegetable dyes may be made from the following:
for deep yellow — the outer skins of onions boiled in water
for red or pink — raw beets boiled in water

Decorating the eggs

For a marbled effect, wrap onion skins around the eggs and tie on with cotton thread before dyeing.

For a tie-dye effect, wrap the eggs in silk material and tie on with cotton thread before dyeing.

For geometric patterns or flower shapes, stick on strips of masking tape before dyeing the eggs.

For yellow, flower-patterned eggs, stick flower petals to damp eggs, cover with onion or shallot skins and tie on with cotton thread before dyeing.

For lined patterns, wind waxed dental floss around eggs before dyeing.

Colored eggs may be painted with more food coloring after the initial coloring has dried.

Chocolate Hollow Easter Eggs Step by Step

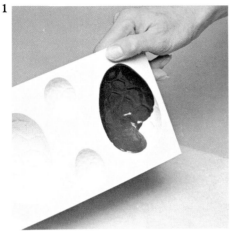

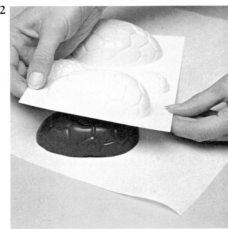

Use candy-making chocolate for these eggs, and prepare it in the same way as for making dipped chocolates (page 154).

The amount of chocolate required depends on the size of the mold. Generally speaking, you will need ½ lb for 2–3 small eggs 4 inches in diameter, 1 lb for larger eggs about 6 inches in diameter, and 1½ lb chocolate for eggs 8 inches in diameter.

1 Pour the prepared chocolate into the Easter egg molds and tilt the molds so that chocolate coats evenly. Place the molds, upside-down, on wax paper and leave to set. Any excess chocolate will drain onto the paper. Reserve this.

2 As the chocolate sets, it will shrink away from the mold so that the egg should fall out easily. Do not pry out with a knife because this will scratch the mold. The inside of the mold has a high gloss so that the finished egg will have a good sheen; if the surface of the mold is scratched, the egg will be dull.

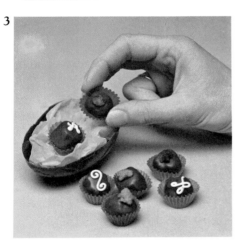

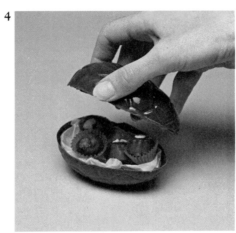

3 Fill one half of the egg shell with chocolates or a small toy or other gift, padding with paper if necessary.

4 Melt the chocolate reserved on the wax paper, or any left in the bowl, and spread over the rims of the two egg halves. Put them together gently. Let set for at least 3 hours or until the egg is firm and the two halves will not come apart.

5 To decorate the egg, melt chocolate in the top of a double boiler. Cool slightly, then put the chocolate into a pastry bag fitted with a star or shell tip. Place the egg, on a square of wax paper, on a drinking glass. This will prevent it from rolling around while you decorate it. Pipe all around the egg where the two halves have been joined together.

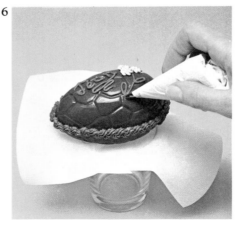

6 Using a plain writing tip, pipe on the name of the person who will receive the egg. Add candy flowers, sticking them to the egg with chocolate.

7 Alternatively, use a thick frosting made from confectioner's sugar and water, tinted with food coloring if desired, instead of chocolate.

8 Make tiny flowers such as roses and stick them to the egg. For children, decorate the egg with an animal or human face, piped on in frosting.

The best way to pack the finished Easter egg is in a tissue-lined box, which will protect it from damage. Smaller eggs may be arranged in a straw basket, on a bed of shredded tissue paper.

7

8

INDEX

Make your home special